MICHAEL MORGAN

DEADLY STORMS
OF THE
DELMARVA COAST

Published by The History Press
Charleston, SC
www.historypress.net

Copyright © 2019 by Michael Morgan
All rights reserved

Front cover: The Grier house in Rehoboth. *Courtesy of the Delaware Public Archives.*

Back cover: Downtown Milton after the 1962 storm. *Courtesy of the Delaware Public Archives*; *inset*: By the middle of the nineteenth century, sand was mounded around Cape Henlopen Lighthouse. *Courtesy of the Delaware Public Archives.*

First published 2019

Manufactured in the United States

ISBN 9781625859389

Library of Congress Control Number: 2019932626

Notice: The information in this book is true and complete to the best of our knowledge. It is offered without guarantee on the part of the author or The History Press. The author and The History Press disclaim all liability in connection with the use of this book.

All rights reserved. No part of this book may be reproduced or transmitted in any form whatsoever without prior written permission from the publisher except in the case of brief quotations embodied in critical articles and reviews.

Contents

Preface   5

1. Assateague: 1524
   Masters of the Wind   9
   A Mixture of Wind, Water and Sand   12
   Our Embarrassment Was a Serious One   14
   Pirates and Ponies of Assateague   18

2. Lewes: 1888
   These Sands Are Alive   22
   Lewes Is a Peculiar Place   27
   Safe from All Winds   29
   Ice Storm: 1888   33

3. Cape Henlopen: Uprooted Trees and Beached Ships
   Moving Sands of Cape Henlopen   46
   The Vagabond Hurricane: 1903   51
   Rehoboth Learns a Lesson   53

4. Ocean City: 1933
   To Take the Salt Air   61
   Assateague: Paradise for Sportsmen   66
   An Inlet Was Born   72

Contents

5. Nature Takes Its Toll
    Great Atlantic Hurricane: 1944 — 78
    Blustery Ladies — 86

6. Ash Wednesday Nor'easter: 1962
    Realization of a Dream — 90
    Assateague: All of the Comforts of Ocean City — 96
    A Few Chunks of Concrete Slab — 102
    Floating Light Poles, Boats and Debris — 108
    Rehoboth: Belies the Imagination — 110

7. The New Reality
    Rebuilding — 119
    Storms after 1962 — 124
    Moving the Ocean — 125
    Three Little Pigs — 130

Bibliography — 133
Index — 139
About the Author — 144

Preface

"Outlying along the Atlantic coast reaching from Cape Charles to Cape Henlopen, from the Chesapeake to the Delaware Bay," the artist Howard Pyle wrote in 1879, "is a continuous chain of islands, corresponding to the Sea Islands of the Carolinas, separated from the mainland by a sheet of water varying in width from a quarter of a mile to seven or eight miles, bearing different names in its more considerable portions, such as Chincoteague Sound, the Broadwater, Sinepuxent Bay, and so forth. These islands, varying in length from less than a mile to two or three leagues, are of two characters, either low and marshy, covered with a thick growth of rank sedge, the refuge of countless millions of fiddler crabs, the brooding place of numberless gulls, marsh hens (Virginia rail), and willits (a variety of snipe), or sandy, and covered with alternate strips of pine glade and salt meadows, on some of which run wild a peculiar breed of ponies, called 'beach hosses' by the natives."

When Pyle wrote his description of the Delmarva coast, the seaside resorts of Rehoboth, Delaware, and Ocean City, Maryland, were barely a half-dozen years old, and the barrier islands were mostly undisturbed by human activity. For eons, the wind and waves had quietly rearranged the Delmarva beaches. In some areas, the littoral currents pushed the sand southward; in other areas, the sand moved northward. In the winter, the prevailing winds robbed the beaches of precious sand, but during the summer, they put it back. There were also larger forces at work. Delmarva sits on one of the earth's tectonic plates that is slowly sinking into the Atlantic Ocean—perhaps as

Preface

Preface

much as a foot per century. In addition, the seas, fed by the melting glaciers and ice caps, are rising as much, if not more. The change in sea level and the prevailing winds have driven the Delmarva coast westward, but this movement occurs so incrementally that it has been largely ignored. What have been noticed are the changes wrought by storms, and these are the subjects of this book, which concentrates on the Delmarva coast from the southern tip of Assateague Island to the northern end at Cape Henlopen.

It would not have been possible to write this book without the assistance of the dedicated people who staff libraries, archives and historical societies. I would like to thank Michael DiPaolo of the Lewes Historical Society and the staffs of the Assateague Island National Seashore, the Snow Hill Public Library and the Julia A. Purnell Museum for their assistance in securing material on the storms that have affected the Delmarva coast. I would also like to thank Randy L. Goss of the Delaware Public Archives for his assistance in securing many of the images that appear in this book. In particular, I would also like to thank Nancy Alexander, of the Rehoboth Historical Society, who suggested this topic, for her patience while I combed through the society's collection of print material and photographs.

I would also like to thank my son Tom and his wife, Karla, for their support and technical assistance. Finally, I would like to thank my wife, Madelyn, for her constant editorial advice and support. She read every word in this book numerous times and spent countless hours correcting my spelling, punctuation and grammar. Without her help and support, this book would not have been possible.

Opposite: This nineteenth-century map shows the Delmarva barrier islands that shielded the peninsula from the Atlantic Ocean. *Courtesy of the Delaware Public Archives.*

CHAPTER 1

ASSATEAGUE: 1524

MASTERS OF THE WIND

"We reached a new country," Giovanni da Verrazano wrote in 1524, when the Italian explorer first saw the barrier islands of North America along the Carolina coast, "which had never been seen by any one, either in ancient or modern times. At first it appeared to be very low, but on approaching it to within a quarter of a league from the shore we perceived...that it was inhabited." The son of a Florentine silk merchant, Verrazano was not impressed with the low, sandy islands that lined the coast, and he sailed farther southward to look for an inlet that would lead to deep quiet water to harbor his ship, the *La Dauphine*. Seeing no appropriate inlet leading to the coastal bay, he turned northward toward the Delmarva coast.

Italian sea captains sharpened their navigation skills by carrying religious Crusaders and merchandise on the Mediterranean Sea; in the late fifteenth century, they ventured into the Atlantic. There, they mastered the art of ocean sailing equipped with a few simple tools—an all-important compass to show direction, a line and chunk of wood dropped over the side to estimate speed, a traverse board to record the course and a simple knowledge of the geometry of the earth and the North Star to determine latitude by simple celestial navigation. Above all, however, experienced navigators relied on their knowledge of the winds: prevailing easterly winds to carry a ship to America, prevailing westerly winds to bring mariners home to Europe, signs of coming storms, strong winds, light winds, winds that would carry a ship to sea and winds to bring it back again. The success of their voyages and their lives were determined by their mastery of the winds.

Educated in France, Verrazano made several sea voyages and became a competent navigator. In 1524, he secured a commission from the king of France to find open water that would lead to the Pacific Ocean and the lucrative markets of the Far East. Instead, he found the barrier islands. Common to the east coast of North America, these low-lying sandy islands were separated from the mainland by a coastal bay and ran parallel to the coast. Verrazano may have encountered European barrier islands that lined the eastern edge of the North Sea from the Netherlands to Denmark, but the spotty islands on the eastern side of the Atlantic Ocean paled in comparison to the sandy barriers that lined the North American coast. When he reached the Outer Banks of North Carolina, the explorer remained so far away from the coast that he mistook the broad expanse of Pamlico Sound for the Pacific Ocean. Continuing northward, Verrazano arrived at the southern tip of the Delmarva Peninsula, where he encountered the line of barrier islands that stretch from Cape Charles to Cape Henlopen. In much of Virginia, the barrier islands are mostly a disconnected series of islands set a considerable distance from the mainland; to this day, they remain undeveloped and sparsely populated. Beginning at the southern tip of Assateague, however, the islands are a broad ribbon of sand divided by a number of inlets and separated from the mainland by narrow coastal bays. Buffeted about by winds and waves, these islands' sands are constantly changing. Inlets appear and disappear, and chunks of the beach become islands only to be reattached to the mainland decades later. Five centuries ago, Verrazano decided to venture into one of the coastal bays. Historians debate the exact locations that Verrazano visited on this voyage, but it appears that he entered Chincoteague Bay from the south and sailed northward until he anchored in the vicinity of Sinepuxent Inlet. Anchoring *La Dauphine* in the calm waters of the coastal bay, Verrazano led several crewmen ashore.

Searching the tall marsh grasses, the French sailors discovered an old woman with two infants; a tall, attractive young woman and an eight-year-old boy shrieking in fear. Verrazano offered the frightened Native Americans some food, which the old woman and the young boy accepted. The young woman, however, threw the food on the ground. The French sailors grabbed the boy and the young woman, but she wrestled free of their grasp and ran, screaming, into the woods.

Assateague: 1524

A monument to explorer Giovanni da Verrazano near the north end of the boardwalk in Rehoboth, Delaware. *Photo by Michael Morgan.*

Having kidnapped a defenseless eight-year-old boy, Verrazano led the landing party back to their ship. After sailing through the Sinepuxent Inlet, Verrazano continued northward, keeping *La Dauphine* far enough from the beach to avoid the dangerous shoals off Fenwick Island. When he reached Cape Henlopen, he was so far from the coast that Verrazano failed to spot the entrance to Delaware Bay and the Great Dune of the cape that was piled high with centuries of sand. He continued northward, where he entered the mouth of the Hudson River and explored the New England coast before the cautious explorer turned *La Dauphine* eastward and headed home.

Verrazano's inability to find a water passage to the East cooled European interest in North America. It was not until the beginning of the seventeenth century that Europeans began to appreciate the value of the mid-Atlantic coast of North America. In 1607, the English established Jamestown colony; and two years later, Henry Hudson renewed the search for a water route across North America. Unlike Verrazano, Hudson sailed closer to shore; in August 1609, he sailed around Cape Henlopen and into Delaware Bay.

At first, the wide mouth of the bay may have given Hudson hope that here was the long-sought passage to China! As he explored the bay, however, he quickly concluded that he was in a great estuary that originated somewhere on the North American continent. Hudson named the estuary the "South River," and he sailed back into the Atlantic Ocean.

A year after Hudson's visit, Samuel Argall arrived off Cape Henlopen. Argall was searching for food for the Jamestown colony when he arrived in the bay. Argall may not have been aware of Hudson's visit the year before, and the English captain decided to name the bay after Lord de la Warr, the governor of the Jamestown colony.

The voyages of Hudson and Argall put Delaware Bay on the map. Although some may have been disappointed that there was no easy water route around North America, others were elated at the vast land available for colonization. Soon, Dutch, Swedish and colonists of other European origin began to settle on the shores of Delaware Bay. Although the location and the outline of the bay were now well known, the shoals and shallows that peppered the bay remained a mystery. Native Americans and other local watermen acquired a practical understanding of the bay's many sandbars. Some of these sailors became pilots who guided ships up the bay from Cape Henlopen to Philadelphia. In the eighteenth century, Joshua Fisher drew upon the accumulated knowledge of the pilots to produce the first detailed chart of Delaware Bay. Three centuries after Giovanni da Verrazano had blissfully sailed by, the discovery of Delaware Bay had been completed.

A MIXTURE OF WIND, WATER AND SAND

When Verrazano looked at the barrier islands, he saw low-lying sand dunes that were punctuated with tufts of grasses, muted trees and shrubs. The explorer did not know—nor did he care—about the geological forces that brought these sandy islands into being. Eons ago, the erosive effects of the retreating Ice Age glaciers on the Appalachian Mountains produced small rock particles that were carried downstream by the Potomac, Susquehanna, Delaware and other rivers, and the particles eventually found their way into the Atlantic Ocean. Further ground into sand by the constant action of the ocean waves, these particles became the miniature building blocks of the barrier islands. Scientists are divided about how this happened. One theory holds that sand accumulated along the coast to form a ridge, and when the ocean broke through and flooded the lowlands behind them, barrier islands were created. Another theory holds that offshore sandbars eventually accumulated enough sand to protrude above the ocean, and when vegetation took root, they became permanent. A third theory maintains that the barrier islands were outgrowths of sand spits that grew from the mainland and became islands when flooded by storms. In all of these theories, the role of sea level rise that resulted from the melting ice caps during the last ice age is believed to have had a great effect on the formation of barrier islands, but it is not fully understood. The barrier islands may have resulted from a combination of causes that were present in some cases and not others. The height of the continental shelf, the amount of sand present and other factors have created a number of distinct islands separated from each other by inlets to the coastal bays. These narrow waterways have not been permanent, as the migrating sand has filled the waterways. Beginning at the Maryland-Delaware border, the barrier islands are so close to the mainland that they are not true islands, because they are connected to the mainland at Rehoboth, Bethany and Fenwick Island. One fact is well known: the Delmarva barrier islands are not permanently in place. They tended to migrate westward, and

In the 1930s, Fenwick Island and much of the Delmarva coast remained undeveloped. *Courtesy of the Delaware Public Archives.*

in some areas, they develop spits to the north and south. In addition, erosive effects of the ocean are exacerbated by storms that have periodically cut and closed inlets.

On his voyage, Verrazano was fortunate that he did not encounter a hurricane or a nor'easter, both storms common to the Delmarva. Unlike hurricanes that are spawned in the warm tropical waters around the globe, nor'easters are native to the eastern coast of North America. Hurricanes are summer storms formed when warm air begins to rise off the ocean and accelerates as it gains altitude, creating a vortex similar to that of water going down a drain. Dependent upon warm water for their strength, hurricanes tend to weaken as they travel northward. Nor'easters can occur at any time of year, and they are formed when a coastal low drifting northward intersects with a high-pressure system moving eastward across North America. The clockwise winds of the high add spin to the counterclockwise winds of the low, and a nor'easter is born. The core of a nor'easter is colder than the surrounding air and is not dependent upon warm water to nourish it. The winds of these coastal storms may reach hurricane force as they lumber up the coast, but the real danger of a nor'easter is water. If the temperature is high enough, a slow-moving nor'easter can dump copious amounts of rain on the coastal region. If the temperatures are below freezing, a nor'easter can create blizzard conditions. In addition, if the storm pounds the coast during high tide, there will be flooding as rain accumulates in the coastal bays, and the excess water, which the wind and tide drive westward, floods the mainland.

OUR EMBARRASSMENT WAS A SERIOUS ONE

When Verrazano visited the Delmarva coast, the Native Americans were only occasional visitors to the beach, and hurricanes and nor'easters eroded dunes, flooded fields and toppled trees; however, there were few beach structures to be damaged by a storm. The Native Americans built permanent homes out of wood and bark with reed mats covering the floor. Some of these structures were small, domelike buildings, and others were rectangular. In addition to constructing permanent inland homes, some tribes visited the coast, where they built similar semipermanent structures. During the hot summer months, they used these "shore homes" near the beach to take advantage of the cool sea breezes. These structures could not withstand a strong thunderstorm, let alone a nor'easter or hurricane. Whenever this happened, however, the Native Americans were able to recover quickly, and they rebuilt their bark and sapling structures. On the north edge of Rehoboth Bay, a Native American encampment was situated about five hundred feet from the beach where there was a level area that ran parallel to the coast. The Native Americans had learned that building too close to the beach invited storm surges to flood their homes and carry away their belongings.

The first European settlers built homes that were a little more substantial than the sapling and bark structures of the Native Americans. The early colonists' homes had wooden frames, wattle and dab walls and thatch roofs. These were able to withstand thunderstorms but remained vulnerable to nor'easters and hurricanes. Within a relatively short time, the Europeans added wooden siding to their homes, and the well-to-do began to build using bricks. Although the colonists sometimes built homes close to creeks and bays to more easily ship their tobacco to market, they shunned the coast, where salt air was detrimental to crops. Consequently, by the middle of the seventeenth century, there were a scattered number of colonists living in the coastal Delmarva area but few settled on the barrier islands, and there were almost no structures within sight of the surf. When a violent storm swept over the peninsula, it damaged structures, but the changes in the barrier islands had little effect. These changes were duly noted, and for the first time, it was evident that the coast was being shaped by these storms. Although the record would remain spotty, these settlers also recorded some of the damaging effects of these storms.

In 1667, a hurricane swept out of the tropics and up the coast. Crossing the Outer Banks of North Carolina, the storm edged eastward and made landfall on the southern Delmarva Peninsula. As the storm crossed the peninsula, the northeast winds and strong tidal surge forced water onto the barrier islands and flooded coastal settlements. The storm

> *overturned many houses, burying in the ruins much goods and many people… blowing many cattle that were near the sea or rivers, into them… whereby unknown numbers have perished, to the great afflication [sic] of all people, few having escaped who have not suffered in their persons or estates, much corn was blown away, and great quantities of tobacco have been lost, to the great damage of many, and utter undoing of others.*

So many trees were uprooted that the fallen trees blocked roads, making it difficult for the colonists to travel. In addition, the ocean rose twelve feet above normal, flooding the coastal area, drowning livestock and forcing the settlers out of their homes. The storm surge was a phenomenon that was to be reckoned with.

The information is not precise, but the damage is typical as to what would follow. Structures in the path of the storm were damaged or destroyed, trees were uprooted, crops were destroyed and the seacoast was eroded. In 1693, a storm crossed the peninsula at Accomack, and the Royal Society of London reported, "There happened a most violent storm in Virginia which stopped the course of ancient channels and made some where there never were any." Known as the Accomack Storm, this event altered the Delmarva shoreline and coastal inlets, changing the coastal topography and cutting new channels through the tidal marshes behind the barrier islands, as well as closing up long-existing channels.

A half-century later, in 1749, a hurricane passed over Cape Henlopen and blew several vessels ashore in Lewes Harbor. Again, the storm created a channel across the neck of Cape Henlopen, damaged several farmhouses and uprooted trees. Within a short time, that damage was also repaired. In September 1775, a hurricane struck the Delaware Bay, and a resident of Philadelphia reported: "We hear of great Devastation in many parts of the country by the washing away of banks, overflowing of meadows, carrying way bridges, mill-dams, stores and spoiling of the roads &c &c." Although the destruction from this storm (and another one the next year) was more severe than that caused by previous hurricanes, the damage was again quickly repaired.

In 1821, the eye of a hurricane passed directly over Cape Henlopen as the storm traveled northward along the coast. Again, the coastal region was battered, but the lack of significant development near the beach saved the coastal region from extraordinary damage and loss of life. Following the Civil War, however, the establishment of a string of ocean resorts that extended from Rehoboth Beach to Fenwick Island introduced a new vulnerability to the coast. Many of the buildings at the resorts were erected on the dunes. With normal high tides licking at their foundations, these structures were particularly vulnerable to the storm surge associated with a hurricane.

Although hurricanes can occur during the summer months, many of the most destructive storms visited the Delaware coast in September. In 1785, a September storm drove the *Faithful Steward* ashore a short distance north of the Indian River Inlet, resulting in the loss of over one hundred lives. Five years later, a three-masted sailing bark, *Friendship*, commanded by Captain Thomas Barlow, encountered a storm near Cape Henlopen in November

1790. A passenger aboard the ship wrote, "Our embarrassment was a serious one. Exposed to a furious tempest in Delaware bay, during a long dismal night, surrounded on every side by shoals and breakers, without a pilot and without sails, we were forced to put the vessel before the wind, which blew in directly for the [Cape Henlopen] lighthouse that shone full in view of us, remarkably bright. We knew not the place or directions of the shoals ahead of us but we were convinced that we could not run long before we met some of them." Despite the valiant efforts of Captain Barlow, the ship was blown onto the beach; the occupants were rescued and taken to Lewes, where they were "treated with great kindness by the inhabitants." Although Barlow may have been embarrassed by beaching his ship, the *Friendship* and all aboard it had survived.

In February 1831, a frigid winter storm with high winds and plunging temperatures swept across southern Delaware. Two schooners and several pilot boats were driven ashore on Lewes Beach, and several houses in Lewes were damaged. A heavy snowfall was accompanied by a monstrous high tide that flooded the marsh at the end of Pilottown Road, drowning a number of cattle and driving water up Lewes Creek, destroying the bridge across the creek and carrying away the wharves.

At Millsboro, the storm drove water from the Indian River across its banks, through the town and into the fields beyond. According to a letter from William E. Waples that was published in the *Baltimore Patriot*,

> *The storm exceeded anything of its kind that ever occurred before, in the memory of any of the oldest inhabitants. A very large amount of property, located on all of our water courses, including cattle, hogs, fences, hay, is swept away. In many instances, houses, the land where the houses stood, the household goods, corn cribs and the contents, were carried off. The tide at this place was four feet higher than ever known, it ran over my mill dam like a heavy surf, carrying everything before it.*

At one point, Waples feared that his furnace, tannery and other properties were being destroyed: "While the storm was raging I gave up all for lost, but am now grateful to say, that the damage is less than I anticipated." When the storm subsided, however, the temperature dropped, and the water in the fields froze. Waples commented on the destruction that was wrought on the Delaware coast: "The whole face of the earth appears to be covered with water, converted into ice, and our principal occupation is to make fires and sit by them."

PIRATES AND PONIES OF ASSATEAGUE

The storms that blew over the Delmarva coast before the Civil War did little apparent damage to man-made structures because there were so few permanent buildings south of Lewes. In a typical example, William Whittington took possession of a grant of one thousand acres on Assateague Island in 1702, and he used most of the acreage for grazing livestock. The deserted nature of the coast drew nefarious individuals, who began to visit the barrier islands, attracted by the isolation that had discouraged more honest settlers. In 1699, Nathaniel Blackiston, the colonial governor of Maryland, received a report that the pirate William Kidd was sailing along the North American coast and that the notorious pirate might attempt to use the coastal bays of Maryland as a hideout. Kidd bypassed the Maryland coast and stopped at Lewes, where tradition has it that he buried treasure in the sands of Cape Henlopen.

A popular Delmarva legend holds that Edward Teach, an imposing figure with a full, dark beard that earned him his infamous nickname, "Blackbeard," followed in the wake of Verrazano and sailed into the coastal bays behind Assateague Island. Some claim that Blackbeard came to bury treasure. More likely, Teach came to repair his ship, take on provisions and visit one of at least a dozen wives that Teach had scattered at various hideouts along the Atlantic coast.

The notoriety of Captain Kidd and Blackbeard increased the chances that they would inspire tales about buried treasure. Charles Wilson, however, was an unknown buccaneer when a letter was discovered that placed him on the sands of Assateague Island with a chest of booty to be buried. According to historians Reginald V. Truitt and Millard G. Les Callette, in 1948, an eighteenth-century letter written by Wilson was found in the lid of an old trunk. The letter stated:

> *To my brother George, there are three creeks lying 100 paces or more north of the second inlet above the Chincoteague Island, Virginia, which is at the southward end of the Peninsula. At the head of the third creek to the northward is a bluff facing the Atlantic Ocean with cedar trees growing on it each about 1 1/3 yards apart. Between the trees I buried in ten ironbound chests, bars of silver, gold, diamonds and jewels to the sum of 200,000 pounds sterling. Go to "Woody Knoll" secretly and remove the treasure.*

Assateague: 1524

The problem with finding any possible treasure hidden by Kidd, Blackbeard, Wilson or any other pirate is that the topography of the Delmarva coast has changed so much. With storms opening and closing inlets along the length of Assateague, it is impossible to locate "the second inlet above the Chincoteague Island" in Wilson's seemingly explicit directions.

Although it was not a pirate ship, the Spanish frigate *Greyhound*, commanded by Captain Daniel Huony, was carrying a significant amount of treasure when a storm drove the ship onto a sandbar a short distance from the Assateague beach on September 6, 1750. The ship's crew was able to ferry several chests of silver to shore. They then muscled the treasure across Assateague Island to the coastal bay, where they loaded the silver into small boats for the trip across the bay to the mainland. By the time the chests had been transferred to wagons, the storm that had firmly mired the *Greyhound* in the Assateague sand had abated. The ship appeared to be in no immediate danger, and the Spanish captain and crew set out for Snow Hill with the chests of silver.

Although this is not mentioned in the surviving records of the *Greyhound* foundering, some people maintain that the ship was carrying a number of horses that swam ashore to Assateague. The horses were allowed to roam freely on the barrier island, where a diet of coarse grasses stunted the growth of their offspring. In 1871, noted travel writer Bayard Taylor arrived on Assateague Island, where he noted: "This is a breeding-place of a race of ponies, which run wild, feeding on the strong beach grass, except once a year, when they are herded, the colts banded with the owners' marks, and the mature animals sold. Those I saw were very handsome creatures, of a bright bay color, and about the size of a Mexican mustang."

Six years after Taylor's visit, the artist Howard Pyle visited Assateague Island. In the April 1877 issue of *Scribner's Monthly*, Pyle wrote, "Thick pine woods cover the island, in virgin growth, here and there opening into a glade of marshy flat, stretching off for a mile or more, called 'the meadows,' where one occasionally catches a glimpse of a herd of ponies, peacefully browsing at a distance." Pyle recounted a twisted version of the *Greyhound* story that held that the ponies were there when the first settlers arrived in the early eighteenth century. According to Pyle, "The tradition received from the Indians of the main-land was that a vessel laded with horses, sailing to one of the Elizabethan settlements of Virginia, was wrecked upon the southern point of the island, where the horses escaped."

Over the years, the notion has persisted that the Assateague ponies descended from horses that arrived on a ship that foundered on the Virginia

Ponies descended from animals that lived on Assateague hundreds of years ago. *Photo by Michael Morgan.*

The annual roundup of Assateague ponies attracts thousands of visitors to Chincoteague, Virginia. *Photo by Michael Morgan.*

part of the island. Several of the barrier islands along the Atlantic coast are home to similar herds of wild ponies, and some speculate that their ancestors may have been horses that farmers had let loose on the islands to graze. Whatever their origin, the Assateague ponies became the primary inhabitants of the island; the horses were seldom bothered by the storms, and they quickly adjusted to changes on the barrier island's beach.

CHAPTER 2

LEWES: 1888

THESE SANDS ARE ALIVE

Henry Hudson sailed the *Half Moon* past the round arc of Cape Henlopen and into Delaware Bay without difficulty. In 1609, Hudson, an experienced English explorer in the employ of the Dutch, surveyed the broad mouth of the bay, the smooth dome of the cape capping the northern tip of the Delmarva Peninsula and the many shoals that lined the bay's bottom. On the shore, Lewes Creek ran from west to east, nearly decapitating the sandy cape from the mainland, where a number of Native Americans, the Siconese, built their domelike wigwams consisting of a wicker frame covered with bark. The Siconese, often grouped together as the Lenape, were part of the Algonquian language group who inhabited the area from the Delmarva Peninsula to New York. Hudson did not stop to investigate the homes of the Siconese, Lewes Creek or the cape. He was looking for a passage to the Pacific Ocean, and he quickly decided that Delaware Bay, filled with shifting sandbars, was not it.

Hudson's brief visit to Delaware Bay induced other Europeans to follow in his wake, and in 1631, the Dutch established the Swanendael colony near Cape Henlopen. The Dutch built a stockade on the high ground on the south side of Lewes Creek near the wigwams of the Native Americans. The Siconese had chosen the site of their homes well. The ground on this side of the creek was high, firm, dry and safe from the high water generated by coastal storms. The creek provided fresh water and a calm harbor for the Europeans to moor their ships. On the north side of the creek, the land on the beachfront of the bay and west of the high dunes of Cape Henlopen was low, sandy and marshy. The Siconese often visited the beach, where they feasted on oysters and discarded the bivalve shells that accumulated into large mounds, some measuring thirty feet high and one hundred feet in diameter.

In 1632, a year after the Dutch settlement had been established, David de Vries, one of the leaders responsible for the establishment of Swanendael, arrived with a shipment of supplies only to discover the charred remains of the colonists' rudimentary buildings, "burnet up. Found lying here and there the skulls and bones of our people and the heads of the horses and cows which they had brought with them." Presumably, a dispute with the Native Americans had led to the destruction of Swanendael and the killing of all the colonists. Before he returned to Europe, however, de Vries noted, "On this side of the river, before the beach, there is something of a sand hill." The sand hill that de Vries described was one of several high dunes that sat on the gentle curve of Cape Henlopen. The largest, towering over seventy feet above the surf, was the Great Dune, the highest dune between Cape Cod and Cape Hatteras. Along the northern shore of the cape, the sand formed a high ridge that was covered with pine trees and coarse grasses. Thick stands of twisted pines and dense patches of coarse grass covered the top of a ridge of sand that was nearly two miles long. Behind the ridge stood a tidal swamp, a dense forest of pine trees and the solid ground of the mainland.

In the seventeenth century, the cape was a smooth curl of sand that began at the Atlantic surf and curved westward in a gentle arch. Once the arch reached the calm waters of Delaware Bay, the sand formed a narrow spit that served as the northern bank of Lewes Creek. At that time, Lewes Creek was wide enough to accommodate most colonial sailing ships, and the gentle curve of Cape Henlopen seemed to present few obstacles to navigation. During colonial times, most captains had little difficulty sailing around the steady curve of Cape Henlopen, but some mariners did have trouble distinguishing the cape from the rest of the Delaware coast. There was no sharp point or other demarcation to indicate where the Atlantic Ocean ended and Delaware Bay began.

Several years after the destruction of Swanendael, Dutch colonists returned to Lewes Creek, and by 1673, the settlement near the northern end of the Delmarva ocean coast had grown into a small village of several dozen inhabitants. Lord Baltimore of Maryland, however, believed that the

Lewes settlers were trespassing on his land, and he dispatched a company of forty armed men to Cape Henlopen to enforce his rule. To discourage unauthorized settlements at the mouth of Delaware Bay, the Marylanders burned all but one building to the ground. After the Marylanders left the smoldering ruins of the town, the resilient residents near Cape Henlopen rebuilt their homes.

Over a decade later, control of Delaware passed into the hands of William Penn, who named the settlement near the cape "Lewes" and selected the sturdy little town as the seat of Sussex County. By the middle of the eighteenth century, the town was home to the county courthouse, a jail, several imposing churches and a few hundred inhabitants. When George Whitefield, the Methodist evangelist, visited Lewes, he commented, "It is not above half so big, more plentiful in prospect of provisions than Savannah in Georgia."

Next to Fenwick Island Lighthouse, this boundary stone marked the eastern end of the border between Maryland and Delaware. *Photo by Michael Morgan.*

When Whitefield visited Lewes, the town had grown to about one thousand inhabitants and was home to bay pilots who, seasoned with an intimate knowledge of the shoals and shallows of the Delaware, guided ships bearing passengers and goods up the Delaware to Philadelphia, the largest and most important city in the colonies. Captains found the mouth of the Delaware Bay treacherous to navigate, and some mariners, like Verrazano, found Cape Henlopen difficult to locate. To remedy this problem, Philadelphia merchants financed a lighthouse constructed of stone and perched on a high, pine-covered dune about a quarter-mile from the surf. On December 5, 1765, the *Pennsylvania Gazette* announced that the Cape Henlopen Lighthouse was finished and, "will be maintained constantly every night from henceforth." Sitting within sight of Lewes, the lighthouse was the first substantial building on the cape, where there were few man-made structures except for the Native American shell mounds on the bayside beach.

The lighthouse, built on a large sand hill between the Great Dune and the ocean, was a boon to mariners navigating the entrance to Delaware

Lewes: 1888

An early print of Cape Henlopen Lighthouse. *Courtesy of the Delaware Public Archives.*

Bay. Although it was not intended to do so, the granite tower also provided a benchmark for the shifting sands of the cape. During the American Revolution, the crew of a British warship spotted cattle grazing on the dunes near the lighthouse. In need of fresh provisions, a small party of sailors was dispatched ashore. The officer in charge confronted keeper John Hedgecock, guardian of the lighthouse, and demanded some of the cattle. Hedgecock reputedly replied, "I'll give you no cows!" The officer, unprepared for Hedgecock's bravado, was speechless. The keeper, however, had plenty to say, and Hedgecock continued, "If you don't get out of here, I'll give you some bullets."

According to tradition, the British officer sheepishly returned to his ship, where he summoned reinforcements. When the landing party returned to the lighthouse, there were no cows to be found. Hedgecock had driven them into the nearby woods. The British feared that there might be bushwhacking Americans hiding in the thick underbrush, and the Redcoats decided that discretion was the better part of valor and quickly left.

Some historians doubt the veracity of Hedgecock's encounter with the British, but the presence of cows grazing on the grasses near the lighthouse had grave implications for the stability of the dunes. When the Cape

By the middle of the nineteenth century, sand was mounded around Cape Henlopen Lighthouse. *Courtesy of the Delaware Public Archives.*

Henlopen Lighthouse was constructed in the 1760s, it stood on a sand hill about a quarter-mile from the surf. The sand dune was anchored in place by deep-rooted trees and an abundance of grasses. Within a few decades of its construction, people began to notice that the dune on which the lighthouse stood was slowly eroding. In the nineteenth century, the hazard of allowing cows to roam around American lighthouses and munch on the dune grass had become quite clear, and the keepers were instructed by the U.S. Lighthouse Board: "In many places, it has been found that cattle, attracted to the light at night, destroyed the strong-rooted grass which hold down sand dunes, and this exposed the lighthouse itself to destruction;

and in such cases a considerable area of land must be fenced in to exclude these beasts." Following the American Revolution, an inspection of the lighthouse revealed that the sand was eroding from the dune on which it sat, particularly during nor'easter gales. Workmen placed gravel around the tower and erected barriers of logs and rail fences to help stabilize the sand, but these measures failed to stop the movement of the sand.

LEWES IS A PECULIAR PLACE

The people of Lewes, however, were not overly concerned about the sand eroding around the base of the lighthouse. The town's residents looked to the past, and they were justly proud of the repulse of an attack by the British during the War of 1812. Thirty years after the war, the travel writer G. Waterman Jr. wrote, "In many respects, Lewes is a peculiar place." He noted,

> *An antiquarian friend pointed out to me a door, still preserved, which had a large hole in it made by a ball from an English vessel during the late war; also a door step, bearing a similar memento of former days and scenes. Along the banks of a small creek on which the town is built may be seen three or four old cannons, which were used in the late war, and some way or other rendered unfit for further service.*

In 1846, three years after Waterman's visit, Solomon Prettyman opened the Ocean House hotel with large, airy and comfortable rooms. In addition, Prettyman built a footbridge over Lewes Creek so that guests at the Ocean House could visit Lewes Beach and enjoy a splash in the bay waters. The popularity of Lewes Beach boomed two decades later when the first railroad line arrived in Lewes in 1869. The railroad enabled vacationers from Wilmington, Philadelphia and other cities to reach Lewes in a matter of hours. In addition, a two-thousand-foot pier was constructed on Lewes Beach, and steamer service was established between the Delaware town and New York. Although the improved transportation brought more vacationers to the new hotels that were springing up on Lewes Beach, the railroad also led the Luce Brothers and S.S. Brown and Company to build fish-processing plants on the bayfront where bathers were enjoying the quiet surf. The two plants extracted oil from menhaden, a fish once so common in mid-Atlantic waters that in 1607, Captain John Smith encountered a school of menhaden "lying so thick with their heads about the water, as for want of nets (our barge driving amongst them) we attempted to catch them with a frying pan." Frequently swimming in the waters near Cape Henlopen, each of the silvery, spotted fish was only a foot long, but they were packed into dense schools that sometimes measured a mile in diameter.

The early settlers had little use for the oily and bony menhaden, but in the nineteenth century, the development of mechanized presses provided an economical method for extracting oil from the fish. A thousand fish yielded about fourteen gallons of oil that was used in lamps, paint and other products. The fish were first boiled in large tanks of water, then a hydraulic press was used to extract the oil and water from the fish. The water and oil were collected in tanks, where the oil rose to the surface and could be skimmed off. Some of the oil, however, remained in the water, and this water

This mid-twentieth-century photo shows the elongated Cape Henlopen, the breakwater to the right of the cape, the fish-processing plants and their piers along the shore and the above-ground buildings of Fort Miles. *Courtesy of the Delaware Public Archives.*

was dumped into Delaware Bay. The combination of decaying fish scraps and putrid water combined to produce an odor that could be overwhelming.

In 1871, the magazine *Manufacturer and Builder* noted that "nine out of every ten of our readers have at some time or other enjoyed a sniff at a barrel of fish-oil. The smell is, doubt-less, one of the few never-to-be-forgotten things of human experience." Most fish-rendering plants were built "as far away from civilization as though in the heart of a wilderness, these works have a certain picturesqueness that is quite pleasing to the artist. But we advise the visitor to go in the winter, as we did, since we will not be responsible for his enjoyment of the perfume." While wild ponies continued to graze on the natural beaches of Assateague Island, at the northern end of the Delmarva Peninsula, the Lewes fish plants gave an aura of nineteenth-century industrialism to Cape Henlopen.

SAFE FROM ALL WINDS

Not only were the fish-rendering plants constructed on the sands of Cape Henlopen, but the waters near the cape were feeling the brunt of nineteenth-century development. On December 17, 1825, the *Niles Register* reported, "The people of Philadelphia are greatly exerting themselves to cause the erection of a breakwater near Cape Henlopen. Some place of security for vessels is, indeed, much wanted; for it is stated that, with the last twenty-three months, no less than thirty vessels have been either sunk or driven ashore, within ten miles of the proposed location of the breakwater; and it is estimated that the loss of revenue to the United States had been equal to the cost of making a harbor for vessels."

In 1826, a report to the House of Representatives listed over 150 vessels that had been wrecked near the entrance to the bay. The report concluded,

> *Place but a shelter at the entrance of the Bay, the commerce of the Delaware will not alone be protected and preserved by it, but that of the whole Coast, daily passing and repassing its Capes, together with foreign vessels, who resort there when overtaken, by accident, at sea. All will find a haven where their crews can be recruited, damages repaired, and their wants fully supplied, secure from mishap or danger; thereby the interests of merchants, and the lives of hundreds of individuals, will be saved from jeopardy or untimely death.*

After some debate, Congress appropriated the funds for the construction of the Delaware Breakwater near Cape Henlopen. In 1829, the first enormous stones—ranging up to six tons—were put in place in what was to become one of the largest peacetime construction projects undertaken by the federal government in the nineteenth century. Using rubble mound construction, the large stones were put into place without benefit of mortar along the bay bottom in a line that was 160 feet wide at its base and tapered at approximately a forty-five degree angle to a crest that was 14 feet above water and 22 feet wide. The ambitious design called for two formidable stone barriers. A 3,600-foot breakwater that began several hundred feet from the beach and extended westward into the bay was intended to shelter ships from the stormy Atlantic. The second barrier was constructed on an angle over 1,300 feet from the western end of the breakwater. This smaller structure was designed to intercept ice flows from the upper reaches of the Delaware Bay and was known as the "Icebreaker." Together, these two barriers were designed to provide a safe anchorage with calm, ice-free water for the hundreds of vessels that sailed in coastal waters.

In August 1839, the initial breakwater off Cape Henlopen was essentially completed when George Coggeshall, aboard the brig *Brilliant*, reported: "At three p.m., we ran in and made good harbor under the lee of the breakwater, where we lay all night, in company with some twenty or thirty sail of ships, brigs and schooners." Coggeshall fully understood why the federal government undertook this immense project: "While lying here at anchor in five fathoms of water, safe from all winds, I fully realized the strong protecting arm of the United States government, in constructing this fine harbor, save the lives of seamen, and the property of all classes of our common country." The artificial harbor was an immediate success, and during storms, dozens of sailing vessels would seek the calm waters behind the breakwater.

In 1872, noted newspaperman and Georgetown native George Alfred Townsend described the breakwater in *Scribner's Monthly*:

> *Here is the great breakwater of stone, still unfinished,—although the work has been in almost continuous progress under our government for more than a third of century,—where sea-going vessels, colliers, and coasters can safely run in from impending storms between Highland Light and Hampton Roads, about three hundred miles. In time of calm, this breakwater is nothing; nearly two long rough sea-walls of toppled stone, raised well above the surface of the waves, and supporting the hut of a lamplighter.*

Lewes: 1888

An early-twentieth-century postcard of the breakwater shows loose rubble construction. *Courtesy of the Delaware Public Archives.*

After the Civil War, the lighthouse, breakwater and fish plants were joined by a number of other structures that helped to monitor the shifting sands on the cape. In the 1870s, the U.S. Life-Saving Service was established by Congress, and in 1876, the Cape Henlopen Life-Saving Station was opened near the ocean beach south of the lighthouse. Eight years later, the Lewes Station was completed on the bay beach. Eventually, stations were

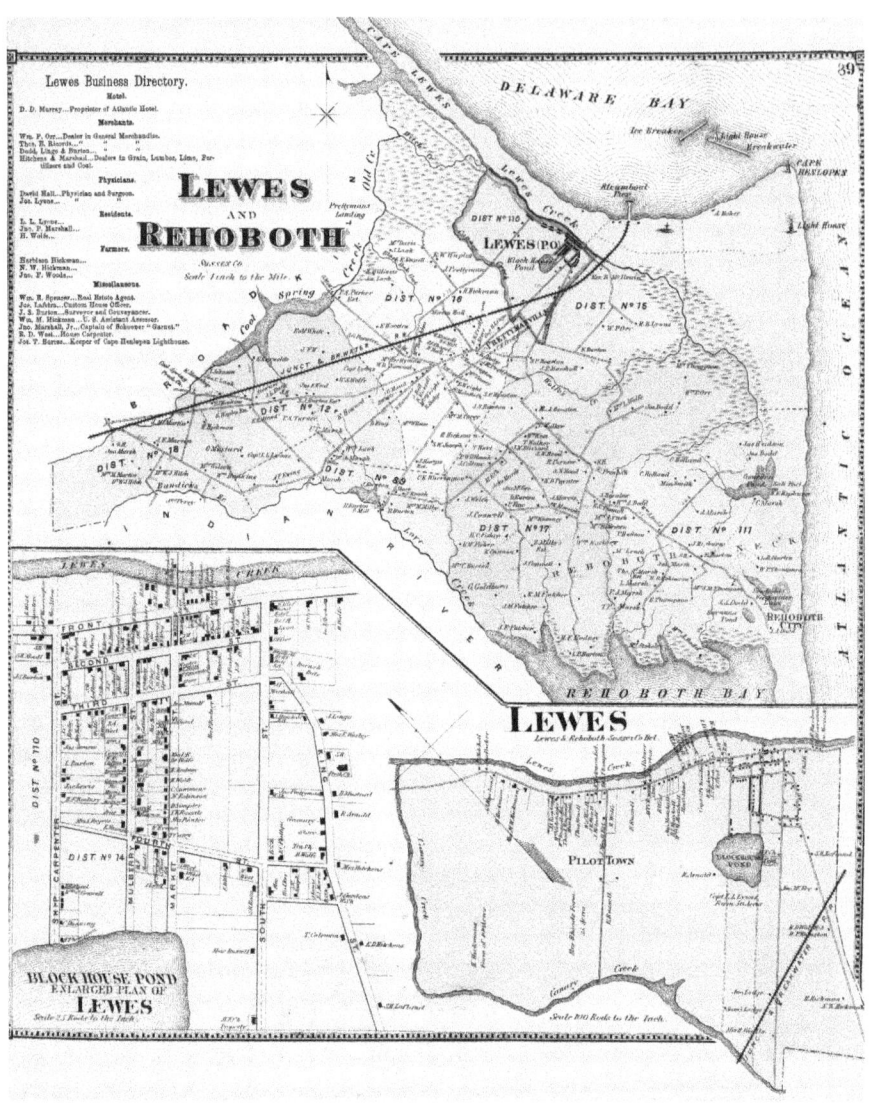

A mid-nineteenth-century map shows the breakwater, icebreaker, Cape Henlopen Lighthouse, the smaller beacon at the tip of the cape and the undeveloped nature of the coast. *Courtesy of the Delaware Public Archives.*

built at Rehoboth Beach, Indian River Inlet, Bethany Beach and Fenwick Island. These stations were in a position to monitor the coast.

In 1884, a quarantine station was established at Cape Henlopen to intercept any immigrant bound for Philadelphia who showed symptoms of an infectious disease. At first, the Delaware Breakwater Quarantine Station's hospital facilities contained a modest six beds and a few workrooms. In 1885, the Delaware Breakwater Quarantine Hospital opened on a rectangular plot of forty-one acres of land fronting the bay. By March 1888, Cape Henlopen was not the deserted sand that it once was, and those who worked in the numerous structures on the cape had a front-row seat for the ever-shifting sands—the natural migration of which had been interrupted by the construction of the breakwater.

Townsend observed,

> *But when the black spot of the distant storm stand up the horizon like Elijah's signal, and the old gossips at Lewes run out their telescopes and look sagaciously ere they make their wagers on the interval before the blow, the water-line is pierced by topsails peeping up from the deep, and barques and schooners crowding sail for refuge. They rise from every point of the water-line and stand in for these friendly piers, where sometimes hundreds of ships, brigs, three-masted schooners, pungies and bay-boats lie together spars entangled, the vast roadstead scarcely equal to its necessities, and on one side the Atlantic, writhing in the grip of storm, howls against the breakwater and dashes over it; while on the other the old, unchanging town of Lewes,—the Plymouth of the races of our Middle States, settled almost continuously since 1638, once worthy of British bombardment, and now unable either to rise or to perish—blinks out at the commerce which is so near and yet so far.*

In March 1888, a black spot of a distant storm appeared on the horizon, and sloops, schooners and other sailing vessels crowded sail to seek refuge at the "friendly piers" of the Delaware Breakwater.

ICE STORM: 1888

Captain John S. Crowell Jr. ordered the sails hoisted, and the crew of the 161-ton schooner *Allie H. Belden* hauled on the lines as the sails inched up the mast and filled with wind and the vessel began to ease out of East Booth

Bay, Maine. In March 1888, Crowell's schooner edged its way past other sailing vessels and smoky steamboats out of the harbor eighty miles north of Portland on Maine's craggy coast. As the *Belden* reached open water, Crowell had more room to maneuver, and when he reached the Atlantic, he set a course southward for Easton, Maryland, on the Chesapeake Bay.

The steamboats that Crowell passed on his way to the ocean were another sign that the age of sail and the masters of the wind were rapidly coming to a close. The perfection of the steam engine in the early nineteenth century enabled steamships to navigate confined waters where reefs, shoals and sandbars presented deadly hazards that all but the most experienced or foolhardy captains avoided. Freed of their dependence on the fickle winds, steamboats could motor against a gale that would have driven a sailing craft onto the beach.

As the *Belden* cruised southward, Crowell sailed past small coastal towns that had once been the backbone of the American shipbuilding industry but lacked the facilities to construct steam engines and steel ships. Shipbuilding became the purview of the big cities—Baltimore, Wilmington, Philadelphia and New York—that boasted ironwork facilities and the mechanics to construct steam-driven ships. The speed and convenience of steamboats made most sailing vessels an anachronism, but shipping merchants who wanted to capture the trade between the Pacific Ocean and the East Coast of the United States built the large sailing clippers, the crowning glory of the square riggers, that did not have to set aside a portion of their cargo space for fuel. Ironically, those firms in the coastal trade found ways to make sailing schooners cheaper to build and operate. The *Allie H. Belden* was one such vessel. The schooner's fore-and-aft rig with the sails bent to the mast instead of spars (as they were in square riggers) allowed the *Belden* to be crewed by six men—fewer than required to furl a single sail on a square-rigged clipper ship. Working from the deck, Crowell's crew worked the sails without having to go aloft. As the *Belden* sailed southward along the Atlantic coast, hundreds of similar craft were navigating the same waters, where a storm was brewing. Crowell, in the tradition of Columbus, Verrazano and other sharp-eyed mariners, saw the storm clouds, and, like the captains of dozens of other vessels, scurried to the protection of the Delaware Breakwater. Steamboat captains, seeing the same dark clouds, blissfully continued on toward their destination confident that they could outrun any high winds and waves they encountered.

In 1888, weather forecasting was an incomplete science. Since forecasters relied on barometric readings taken on shore and on ships at sea and telegraphed to a collection center, useful weather information could be compiled after a storm abated, but, often, those trapped in a tempest had little idea of when the storm would subside. It was not until a year after the late-winter nor'easter that swept along the Atlantic coast that the *Annual Report of the United States Life-Saving Service* was issued and stated: "The terrible tempest of wind and snow that swept over a large portion of the United States on March 12, 1888, will not soon be forgotten, and was in many respects the most remarkable in the country's history of elemental disturbances." Gathering force as far west as the Rocky Mountains and coursing eastward, a high-pressure system with subfreezing temperatures made its way south of the Great Lakes toward the Atlantic coast. In the vicinity of Cape Hatteras, the high-pressure system carried cold temperatures and strong winds when it collided with a moisture-laden low-pressure system lumbering along the coast. The two systems combined to create a nor'easter with high winds and frigid temperatures that resulted in sleet and snow that threatened ships along the coast for days. According to the report from the Life-Saving Service:

> *It was felt with greatest severity in the Middle Atlantic States, though throughout the entire stretch of country and coast, reaching beyond the Canadian border, the effects were of nearly equal magnitude. The sleet and snow blew in straight streaks through the air and mounted into tremendous drifts wherever obstructed. In fact, the quantity of snow that fell would of itself have made this storm without precedent, even had it occurred in the midst of winter.*

Along the coast, the *Democratic Messenger*, published in Snow Hill, Maryland, reported, "But few persons in this [community recalled] ever seen such weather as [was experienced] during the early [part of the past] week." Sunday, March 11, was windy and rainy along the coast, and few people anticipated the severity of the approaching storm. As the center of the nor'easter approached, the wind whipped "about the windows and around [the chimney] tops" so strongly that Snow Hill "rocked like a cradle." One house shook so much as "to produce sea sickness" in the inhabitants.

As the storm moved northward, temperatures continued to drop. Inland, the rain turned to snow, which blocked roads and suspended train service. Miles of telegraph and telephone wires were torn from their poles, and normal means of communication were cut off. The ordinary rhythms of life—from big cities like New York to small towns like Milford,

Delaware—were abruptly brought to a complete standstill. According to the annual report of the Life-Saving Service, "Desolation and suffering were marked on every hand. Many lives were lost, and doubtless hundreds more were shortened. Though all the dire effects of the storm can never be known, it is certain that they were the most disastrous ever experienced with the same limits." In Delaware, the *Smyrna Times* reported that in New York:

> *Every sort of business and industry had been almost paralyzed, street railways were still impassable; snow was piled up to a height of 10 to 15 feet in many places; many of the streets were absolutely impassable for teams; and, worse than all, the city's food supply was running short. Milk and vegetables were approaching famine princes and coal $15 per ton, not because there was not coal enough in the yards but because of the labor delivering it.*

As the storm gained strength, experienced mariners steered for the Delaware Breakwater, which offered some protection against the growing waves of the burgeoning blizzard. By the time the storm had unleashed its fury, several dozen vessels collected behind the stone barrier of the breakwater. Captain Crowell, fresh from his voyage from Maine, dropped the *Allie H. Belden*'s starboard anchor at 11:00 a.m. on March 11 amid the ships that huddled near Cape Henlopen.

On Cape Henlopen, overlooking the scores of vessels anchored behind the breakwater, Life-Saving Service surfmen trudged through the wind and freezing rain across the sand on their normal patrols. The keepers of the four stations on the northern half of the Delaware coast (Lewes, Cape Henlopen, Rehoboth Beach and Indian River Inlet) were all long-term local residents, as were a great many of the surfmen that they led. Writing in the *Organization and Methods of the United States Life-Saving Service*, Sumner Kimball, the general superintendent of the service, declared that the keepers "are the captains of their crews; exercise absolute control over them." New York congressman and staunch supporter of the Life-Saving Service Samuel Sullivan "Sunset" Cox pointed out, "A principal reason for the efficiency of this service is, that men who know the coast and its local navigation, its currents, eddies, and bars—fishermen and surfmen—have been its agents. No 'amateurs' have been employed."

Cox, known for his colorful language (and having earned his nickname for an editorial he wrote describing a "flaming sunset" after the passing of a major storm), described the work of a surfman:

Lewes: 1888

A collection of sloops and schooners huddled behind the breakwater during the ice storm of 1888. *Courtesy of the Delaware Public Archives.*

> *It is to his ready hand, sagacious eye, and equipoised head that we mainly owe the triumphs of the service. He acts under strict discipline, as well in his "beat" upon the shore as in his venture through the surf. The patrol system is directed by rigid rules. At night, and in fog, the surfman at great peril, patrols the beach from two to four miles on each side of his station. His eye is on the sea. His bears a lantern for his guide, and a Coston light [flare] with which to warn, by its red flaring flame, the endangered vessel, or to signal those already stranded.*

The unofficial motto of the Life-Saving Service—"You have to go out, but you don't have to come back"—would be tested.

The blinding wind and numbing cold of a winter storm did not deter the surfmen from their patrols, and hundreds of patrols ended with the surfmen returning to their station with nothing to report. In addition to watching the drills at the life-saving station, a visitor to the Delaware beach once observed a surfman making his nightly patrol and recalled:

> *We were strolling homeward and came up with the dark, trim figure. "Oh, you've no idea," said this young perambulating beacon, "from looking at this beach tonight what it can be in winter! I've waded along here sometimes*

when the wind and tide were as high and the darkness so thick that I didn't know when I passed those hotels; there's no use to carry a lantern, it only makes lights and shadows that mislead, the eyes gets accustomed to finding the line of the surf better without it."

On that Sunday night, the wind shifted to the northwest and increased to hurricane force. The temperature dropped, and the rain changed to snow. Aboard the *Belden*, Crowell dropped the port anchor, but he had trouble keeping the schooner in place. After midnight, Crowell discovered that the schooner was dragging both anchors, and at 2:30 a.m., the *Belden* struck a sandbar. The vessel began to be battered by the heavy waves, some of which broke over the grounded schooner. Fearing that the schooner would be pounded to pieces, Crowell ordered the ship's boat to be lowered, but a heavy wave broke the line that secured the boat to the schooner. The *Belden*'s crew watched as the boat drifted away, and according to Crowell, "We then took to the main rigging to save our lives. All this time it was a thick snow storm, and the wind still blowing with hurricane force, and very cold."

Captains of other vessels behind the supposed safety of the Delaware Breakwater were also finding that the winds began to rip at the vessels with such force that their anchors could no longer hold them in place. The high wind slammed vessels together, splintering hulls and entangling rigging. By morning, the water around Cape Henlopen was littered with debris from wrecked ships. Some sailing vessels that managed to avoid colliding with other ships had their masts snapped by the high winds, and the crews of these vessels struggled under a canopy of tangled spars, rigging and snow to keep their ships afloat. The surfmen of the Lewes station need not look far to discover not one or two but dozens of vessels in distress.

Alerted by the night patrols of the disaster behind the breakwater, John A. Clampitt, the keeper of the Lewes Station, prepared his surfmen for the daunting day ahead. The Clampitt family had settled in Sussex County at the end of the seventeenth century, when Lewes was hardly more than a hamlet nestled in the lee of Cape Henlopen. John's father was a Delaware Bay and River pilot, a profession that required a thorough knowledge of the winds and shifting sands. John, however, did not follow in his father's footsteps; instead, he became a carpenter, and when the Life-Saving Service was established, he enlisted as a surfman. In 1883, he was promoted to keeper of the Lewes station.

On March 12, 1888, when Keeper Clampitt led his surfmen out of the station and into the howling nor'easter, the force of the gale was so great

Lewes: 1888

A two-masted sailing vessel was just one of the many vessels driven ashore or wrecked by the ice storm of 1888. *Courtesy of the Delaware Public Archives.*

that the sand and sleet whirling in their faces so cut and buffeted them that they were forced to lie on the ground and crawl on their hands and knees back to the station. Half an hour later, the weather lulled somewhat, and the surfmen again set forth. A few hundred yards offshore, they spotted the *Allie H. Belden* fast aground with five men clinging to the rigging. During the night, the schooner's steward could no longer maintain his hold on the lines, and he fell into the churning waters and drowned.

At daybreak, Crowell saw that the stranded schooner was near the Lewes Life-Saving station, and he saw "men were running to and fro" on the beach, where Clampitt ordered the surfmen to use the Lyle gun to fire a line to the stranded schooner. Aboard the *Belden*, Crowell "saw a rocket line coming towards us. They fired five different times, but the wind blew with such force they could do nothing for us."

As the Lewes surfmen tried in vain to string a line to the doomed schooner, another of the sailors fell from the rigging and drowned. Around noon, the stays supporting the schooner's mainmast parted, and the mast fell overboard. Fortunately, Crowell and the three remaining sailors were able to scramble into the rigging of the foremast, where they climbed into the crosstrees high above the raging waves. Seeing that the situation about the *Belden* was desperate, Clampitt decided to launch the surfboat. The winds were so strong, however, that the surfmen manning the oars were quickly exhausted. After nine hours of grueling work in the icy storm, the surfmen reached the stricken schooner, where they rescued Crowell and the three sailors who had clung to the rigging, where they had been exposed to the snow and wind for twelve hours. The four other cold but alive men from the schooner were ferried ashore.

While the surfmen from the Lewes station struggled to reach the *Allie H. Belden*, Keeper Theodore Salmons, another longtime Delaware resident, arrived from the Cape Henlopen station with several of his surfmen. At daylight, a surfman on patrol had returned to the Cape Henlopen station and reported wreck debris on the beach north of the station. Salmons mustered the surfmen, who began to make their way toward the cape. The temperature had fallen, and the heavy rain had turned to snow. James Merryman, chief inspector for the Life-Saving Service, described a similar trek in *Harper's Monthly Magazine*:

> *A march of four or five miles through the soft sea-sand is a task at any time; what is it in the fury of winter storm? The prevalent strong winds, which must be encountered in one direction or other of the beat, drive before them rain, snow, hail, and sleet, or oftener sharp sand, which cuts the face until, smarting with pain, the patrolman turns and walks backward for relief.*

According to the official report of the Life-Saving Service, the surfmen struggled through the storm "with the greatest difficulty against the snow and driving sleet to the point of the cape, where they discovered, as the weather temporarily lightened up, several vessels in distress."

Salmons and the surfmen discovered Clampitt and the Lewes crew doing their utmost to rescue those aboard the *Allie H. Belden*, and the keeper of the Cape Henlopen station borrowed a short-line and hurried to the nearest stranded vessel, the pilot boat *Enoch Turley*. Salmons was able to reach the *Turley*'s crew using the breeches buoy. As the surfmen of the Lewes and Cape Henlopen stations continued their rescue efforts, they were joined by Keeper Thomas Truxton and the surfmen of the Rehoboth Beach station. Truxton, another longtime resident of Lewes, was a member of a great seafaring family and the first keeper of the West End light on the breakwater. Truxton was appointed to be the keeper of the Rehoboth station, situated in what is now Dewey Beach, in 1878. When he learned of the growing disaster at the breakwater, the crew of the Rehoboth Beach station marched across six miles of storm-swept beach to join the other surfmen in their rescue efforts. Temperatures had continued to fall overnight, the surface of the water was freezing and the stranded vessels were becoming encrusted with ice.

As the three crews of surfmen ferried the crews of damaged and stranded vessels ashore, they were reinforced by the arrival of Keeper Washington Vickers of the Indian River Inlet Station, and two of his surfmen started out through the wind and snow toward the cape. Washington A. Vickers, born in 1842, was raised in Seaford; at the start of the Civil War, he slipped south to join the Confederate army. Vickers was wounded at the battle of Gettysburg, and following the Civil War, he enlisted as a surfman in the Life-Saving Service and was stationed at Hog Island in Virginia. Later, he transferred to the station on Assateague Island, where he remained for several years. Vickers returned to Delaware when he moved to the Indian River Life-Saving Station, where he was promoted to keeper.

The wrecked superstructure of the *Lizzie Crawford* showed that even steam-driven vessels could not escape the fury of the storm of 1888. *Courtesy of the Delaware Public Archives.*

When the three men completed their fourteen-mile trek up the coast, they spotted the stranded boat and the struggling surfmen. Vickers immediately went to the marine hospital, where they recruited several men and then hurried back to the beach. The men's combined force was able to free the boat from the clutches of the ice and haul it ashore. According to the official report: "In all likelihood, the men in the boat would have perished had not the surfmen from Indian River Inlet put in an appearance when they did." By this time, night had again fallen, and rescue operations ceased for the day.

At daybreak on March 14, the weather had moderated, but a strong breeze continued to blow snow squalls across the bay, where nearly every craft in the harbor was now fast in the ice. As soon as it was light enough, the surfmen of the Lewes and Cape Henlopen stations resumed rescue operations, which continued throughout the day. By this time, several dozen men from Lewes had arrived on the beach to assist the surfmen. By the end of the day, most sailors had been ferried ashore when nightfall again interrupted the rescue efforts. On March 15, four days after the storm had started, the last sailors were finally brought ashore.

The Great White Hurricane, as the blizzard of 1888 was sometimes called, damaged or destroyed thirty-five vessels near Cape Henlopen. Inland, cities and towns were buried under mountains of snow, and the blizzard so paralyzed New York City that the storm helped convince some of that city's leaders of the need to build a subway system. In Delaware, the snow accumulated to prodigious depths. In some areas of Milford, twenty miles northwest of Lewes, six feet of drifted snow filled the streets.

At the breakwater, several sailors died from exposure, but nearly two hundred crewmen from about two dozen ships were rescued. Aboard the *Allie H. Belden*, two sailors died, but Captain Crowell and three others were rescued. When the weather cleared, Crowell went to inspect the *Belden*, but there was nothing to be seen except the battered hull of the schooner at the water's edge. There was little interest in saving the schooner's cargo of ice.

Fifteen months later, in September 1889, a hurricane came out of the tropics and slammed into the mid-Atlantic coast. As in 1888, captains of dozens of coastal sailers correctly read the warning signs and hurried to the protection of the Delaware Breakwater. At Assateague Island, the rain filled Sinepuxent Bay and combined with the erosive effect of the high ocean waves to create several low inlets across the beach. At Ocean City, the *Democratic Messenger* reported, "the water rose higher and higher at each tide thereafter until it swept through the lower floors of the cottages." Water inundated the beach, and "the bath houses were all torn down by

Lewes: 1888

After the 1888 storm had passed, a young man relaxed in front of the Mullikin Brothers drugstore in downtown Milford, Delaware. *Courtesy of the Delaware Public Archives.*

The ice storm of 1888 piled snow high in the streets of Milford, Delaware. *Courtesy of the Delaware Public Archives.*

This overturned sailing vessel may have been the *Allie H. Belden. Courtesy of the Delaware Public Archives.*

the fury of the breakers and washed away, while the waves were washing over the porches of the Atlantic Hotel, breaking in the doors of Congress Hall and damaging the Atlantic's pavilion." According to the *Democratic Messenger,* "Many shade trees [in] Snow Hill were shorn of their branches and in some instances uprooted. The electric light wires were torn down in many places and coal oil lamps had to be brought in use." The high winds generated by the hurricane led the newspaper to proclaim "that this storm is the worst for at least thirty years and destruction to life and property is now inestimable. The loss of life in Delaware bay by the storm has been almost as heavy as during the great blizzard of March 1888." The Delmarva coast was littered with wrecked vessels, and an estimated thirty-five people lost their lives.

After the twin storms of 1888 and 1889, a second, longer breakwater was built near Cape Henlopen a mile north of the original stone barrier. The second breakwater was completed in 1901 and created the National Harbor of Refuge, where vessels would be "safe from all winds." The continued decline in the number of commercial sailing vessels, coupled with the rise of steamship vessels that were able to power away from storms, mitigated the need for the calm waters created behind the new breakwater. The missed lesson of the storms of the 1880s was not the need for a National Harbor of Refuge but changes in the way the sand was carried around Cape Henlopen. The old breakwater interrupted the movement of water-bearing sand around the cape, and the new Harbor of Refuge exacerbated this change, causing Cape Henlopen to develop an elongated sandspit at its northern end. In addition, the westward migration of the coast continued.

CHAPTER 3

Cape Henlopen: Uprooted Trees and Beached Ships

MOVING SANDS OF CAPE HENLOPEN

After the blizzard of 1888 and the hurricane of 1889, the Delmarva coast experienced more than a decade of relative calm, but the wind and tides continued to take their tolls on the coast. The "something of a sand hill" that David de Vries observed in 1632 continued to migrate inland. In 1890, maritime writer John R. Spears described the effect of the wind-driven sands of Cape Henlopen in *Scribner's Magazine*: "A mammoth wave of sand, that towers aloft like a sea-wave even curling over in places like a huge breaker, is rolling inland irresistibly, and lacking only the elements of speed in its career to carry such terror to the hearts of the inhabitants, as is inspired by the sea-waves that follow an earthquake." In the early nineteenth century, the dune appeared to be securely anchored in place. Spears reported, "According to gray-haired observers living near Henlopen, the sand wave…was fifty years ago, simply a great dune or ridge lying along the northerly side of the cape. The foot was washed by the waves whenever a northeast gale was blowing; its crown covered with twisted pines interspersed with patches of coarse grass."

In 1845, a government engineer surveyed the cape and determined that the top of the dune was seventy-two feet above the sea. Behind the two-mile-long ridge of sand, a tidal swamp stood between the sands of Cape Henlopen and the solid ground of the mainland. A dense forest of towering

Cape Henlopen: Uprooted Trees and Beached Ships

The sands of Cape Henlopen inundated the forest to the west of the dunes. *Courtesy of the Delaware Public Archives.*

pine trees stood on the landward edge of the swamp. When work began on the Delaware Breakwater in the early nineteenth century, residents of Lewes noticed a change in the sand ridge. Northerly winds began creating dense storms that sent clouds of coarse sand whipping across the cape. The sand was lifted from the northern face of the ridge and carried up and over the crest by a flood of wind-blown sand. On the Great Dune, easterly winds also lifted the grains of sand and, like a wave, drove it westward. Effectively, the Great Dune was moving inland, away from the beach; as it did so, the ocean was making its way westward.

With each breeze, the sand wave from the Great Dune continued its move inland and inundated anything that stood in its path. Any people who ventured on to the dune when the wind was high had to cover their faces with handkerchiefs to avoid the choking sand. The constant sea breeze drove the sand across the top of the ridge and deposited it in the lee of the dune. As the dune shifted inland, the trees that once thrived on the crest of the ridge were stripped of most of their branches, leaving ghostly trunks taller than a person. Trees in the low ground on the landward side of the ridge were inundated by a flood of windblown sand, as the ridge had become a relentless slow-motion wave that was literally rolling in from the sea.

According to Spears, "The ditches where the tides had gurgled in and out were filled. The tree-covered ridges that marked the swamp had the sand piled over them, and then the substantial forest on the low plateau beyond the swamp was reached, and the most interesting epoch in the history of the wave began." Where the trees stood wide apart with little or no underbrush, the sand was like lava flowing between and around the trunks. In places where there was underbrush and a dense thicket of interlaced limbs, Sears wrote, "the wave rolled up before them as the Red Sea rose up against the hosts of Pharaoh." The sand rose higher and higher among the trees until the crest of the sand wave was reached and toppled over, burying the tree as a sea wave buries a rock. With every breeze, sand was driven among the trees, and when storms slammed the coast, incalculable amounts of sand flooded the forest. According to Spears, "The great trees that seemed capable of resisting every force that nature might bring against them struggled against fate, strove to put forth new shoots and branches above the rising tide, reaching out as if for succor, grew faint in the struggle, turned their green leaves to yellow, the yellow to black, and so gave up and died pitifully."

The shifting sands of the cape also undermined the foundation of the Cape Henlopen Lighthouse. When it was constructed in 1765, the builders placed the lighthouse near the end of the stable ridge that ran across the northern face of Cape Henlopen. For years, the lighthouse stood a quarter-mile from the surf amid the trees that covered the top of the dune. During the nineteenth century, the blowing sands beat upon the lighthouse and the keeper's home. Fine grains were thrown against doors and windows until they sifted through small cracks into the interior of the house, where they covered rugs, bedding, bureau drawers and clothes-closets. No amount of weather-stripping or endless sweeping could keep the sand out. In the windbreak created in the lee of the keeper's house, the sand piled so high against the back of the building that children entered the building through the second-story windows. The great sand wave rose up like a slow-moving, surging wall of water bearing down on the oil-house until it broke over the building and buried it. When the accumulated sand made the keeper's house unlivable, Spears wrote,

> *Uncle Sam built a new one, placing it well up the face of the sand-wave. But it did not protect it wholly, for the crest advanced steadily, until it passed the light-tower and gathered around the new dwelling, burying its*

Cape Henlopen: Uprooted Trees and Beached Ships

verandah and half the lower story, and forming about the tower a crater, thirty feet deep on one side, that is a most curious spectacle to the visitor.

The traveling dunes of Cape Henlopen moved more than fifty feet per year, and they became one of the most remarkable features of the coastal region. In addition to the "walking" dunes, the beach sands near the cape were also on the move. The construction of the original Delaware Breakwater and the outer breakwater that became known as the Harbor of Refuge had interrupted the natural flow of the currents that carried sand around the smooth hump of the cape. The slower-moving currents dropped the sand north of the cape, which began to develop a spit that extended into the mouth of the bay.

Two years after Sears published his observations of the moving sands of Cape Henlopen, artist Howard Pyle, who was a frequent visitor to the coast, published an illustrated article entitled "Among the Sand Hills" for the September 1892 issue of *Harper's Monthly*. Pyle wrote, "Cape Henlopen is a level hook of sand covered with scrub bushes. Within the hook lies the perfect curve of a sheltered harbor." Pyle, who was deeply interested in the history of the coast, knew that shifting sands were not confined to the land but also were constantly on the move in the waters near the cape. He wrote: "Long cruel bars and shoals stretch out their fingers under the water. Scores and hundreds of vessels that have weathered many a bitter storm die here within the very sight of the goal. The level point of the cape is strewn thick with bleaching ribs and broken bones of the poor lost things." Pyle echoed the observations of Spears:

> *Back of the Cape lie not only the strange white lifeless hills and valleys, and the dark skirt of pine woods with its circling shadows, hot and dry and still, but dense jungles and tangled wildernesses; and hidden gloomy swamps of stagnant waters inhabited by strange wild creatures; and here and there lonely little lakes of fresh water blooming, in the midst of the grotesque dark surroundings, with field of white lilies.*

Not only was Pyle enthralled by the sands of Cape Henlopen, he was also inspired by the stories of pirates who once roamed the coast:

> *The ceaseless whispering of the sands might…perhaps, tell of buried treasures, and of strange things seen and done in the white solitudes of its hills and valleys. For in old days, it is said, great and famous pirates*

This rare photograph shows the forest of dead trees killed by the shifting sands of Cape Henlopen. *Courtesy of the Rehoboth Historical Society.*

used to haunt the cape and its sand hills, and chests and barracoes were mysteriously buried, mostly at night, among the black shadows of the pines, or in the white sloping face of the sand.

Pyle concluded, "Here and there a stark gray tree trunk, already dead in the clutch of the oncoming death, reaches helpless skeleton arms up into the air. Each is an empty hollow shell of bark; each is soulless and void of life, excepting, perhaps, for a nest of woodpeckers or of mice—squalid metempsychosis of the spirit of the pine trees."

Sears and Pyle recognized that the sands on the northern tip of the Delmarva Peninsula were constantly in motion. In fair weather, the sands traveled slowly but steadily. When the skies darken and the barometer drops, signaling the arrival of a major storm, the shifting sands of the coast move with astounding speed.

THE VAGABOND HURRICANE: 1903

By the early years of the twentieth century, seaside cottages, hotels and boardwalks lined the Delmarva sands. Where there were once only scrub-covered dunes, there were now hundreds of wooden structures at Lewes Beach, Rehoboth and Ocean City that were exposed to storm-whipped wind and water. In September 1903, a tropical hurricane, born over a thousand miles east of the Bahamas, crawled through the broad waters of the Atlantic until it curved northward along the Outer Banks of North Carolina and ran up the Delmarva coast. Nicknamed the "Vagabond Hurricane" for its unpredictable behavior, the storm swept past Assateague Island and ripped into Ocean City. According to the *Democratic Messenger*, "At Ocean City, almost every building was damaged." The roofs were blown off from the pavilions of Gilbert B. Cropper and J.D. Rayne, several hotels and other structures. Beach cottages, the boardwalk and the tracks of the Baltimore, Chesapeake & Atlantic Railway Company that ran across the coastal bay into the resort were damaged. The Plimhimmon and Atlantic Hotels escaped unharmed, but the Congress Hall was reported to be a total wreck. At the south end of town, most of the boats of the pound fishermen were smashed, and their nets were carried away in the storm.

Melville Church and his family from Washington were staying in a cottage when they decided to evacuate. According to the *Democratic Messenger*, "The occupants tied themselves together with ropes and just as they were about to step into the water which was waist deep around their cottage, the back porch on which they were standing gave way....Four sturdy men dragged them from the water."

A short distance inland, a few buildings lost their roofs and "the large brick building of Will J. Collins, carriage manufacturer and wheelwright, was in the center of extreme violence, the building was utterly demolished." After the storm ended, there were piles of debris mingled with broken carriages, machinery, bricks and mortar, timber and other fragments scattered throughout the resort. A short distance inland, the *Democratic Messenger* reported, "From all sections of the county come reports of the havoc wrought in every step of the storm's path." In orchards, trees were stripped of their fruit; in corn fields, stalks were leveled, and roads were obstructed by fallen trees.

As the storm moved into Delaware, the story was much the same. According to the *Delaware Pilot*, "Corn standing the fields was blown over and fodder was much damaged....One would naturally suppose that tomatoes would be hurt badly but such is not the cases; tomatoes fared best of all." The *Delaware Pilot* reported that "Lewes got off with a number uprooted trees, and wrecked buildings but probably the most serious damage was the blowing down of the smoke-stack at the power house which caused the town to be left in darkness." The bayside piers sustained some damage, and the telephone and telegraph lines were broken, leaving Lewes cut off from quick communication with the outside world.

The three-masted schooner *Hattie A. Marsh*, of New London, slammed into the new outer breakwater (the Harbor of Refuge). The vessel struck the broadside to the rocks, and the heavy seas broke continuously over the disabled schooner. Five of the crew and the captain took shelter in the lee of the deckhouse, but when a large wave washed the deckhouse overboard, the men were carried into the sea. The mate and a seaman, the only surviving crewmen, managed to crawl up the rigging clear of the force of the heavy seas. These two men were rescued by the steam pilot boat *Philadelphia*. Another small schooner, the *Seabird*, sank inside the old breakwater, and a sloop, *Maud S*, was deposited high and dry on Lewes Beach opposite the Ocean House. The crews of these two vessels safely reached shore. Although the storm damaged several coastal vessels, the Vagabond Hurricane demonstrated that the increased development of the coastal area put property on the shore at risk.

REHOBOTH LEARNS A LESSON

From the very first, the people of Rehoboth were in love with the sea. As in Ocean City, Maryland, most other Atlantic seaside towns were built on barrier islands, and the major streets ran parallel to the beach; but at Rehoboth, the mainland ran down to the surf, and town was laid out somewhat like a triangle, with its base at the beach and its two longer sides extending inland to the grove where camp meetings were held. The founders of the resort, the leaders of the Methodist Camp Meeting Association, envisioned early vacationers at Rehoboth enjoying the regenerative effect of the sea breezes and the soothing sounds of the waves and attending open-air church services in the grove. The town's principal streets radiated from the camp meeting grove at the inland point of the triangle toward the beach, where they met at a street named, appropriately enough, Surf Avenue, which ran parallel to the ocean. At the time, Surf Avenue seemed to be a great idea. The unpaved street provided a convenient promenade for people, horses and carriages to take a leisurely stroll, get a good look at the ocean and enjoy the cooling sea breezes. In the 1880s, a boardwalk eight feet wide and only a quarter-mile long was constructed between Surf Avenue and the beach. In addition, the hotels and beachfront homes on Surf Avenue had a commanding view of the ocean. What the founding fathers of Rehoboth did not expect, however, was that storm-driven ocean waves would sometimes inundate Surf Avenue, and ships would one day ride up almost to the front porches of the buildings on the oceanfront street.

The new resort's main street was Rehoboth Avenue, which ran from the grove to the beach; Surf Avenue, with its commanding views of the ocean, became a favorite spot for beach homes. Writing in the April 1876 edition of the *Rehoboth Beacon*, Reverend Enoch Stubbs commented, "The distance of the camp meeting grove (3/4 mile) from the beach, where the hotel and almost all of the cottages are located, and the absence of any efficient conveyance to and fro rendered it impossible for those to be very closely indentified with the services who were not tented in the grove."

At first, vacationers rode in their carriages along Surf Avenue, where they admired the view of the beach and the breakers. When the newfangled horseless carriages were invented, they, too, were driven along Surf Avenue. In the early twentieth century, an expanded boardwalk was built, and gaslights provided a bright walkway for strolling vacationers who wanted to enjoy the sound of the pounding surf and the refreshing evening

Rehoboth's Surf Avenue in its heyday. *Courtesy of the Rehoboth Historical Society, Paul Preston Davis Collection.*

breezes. At first, the gaslights were turned off at 11:00 p.m. Eventually, electric lights were installed, and the boardwalk remained crowded with strollers until the early hours of the morning. A promotional brochure proclaimed, "It is one mile long and sixteen feet wide, with a substantial hand rail, and is lighted by gas the entire length. Here during the season may be found representatives of the wealth, beauty and fashion of our large cities, and while the walk may be crowded, it is always a well-behaved crowd." There were, however, no crowds on the boardwalk when a fierce winter storm struck the resort in January 1914.

Rehoboth was still recovering from a storm that had swept up the coast the week before when the wind began to rise and the waves started eroding the sand from the beach. Horn's Pavilion and pier, the centerpiece of resort activity during the summer months, was pounded by the waves until the planks of the pier gave way. Although the underpinnings of the pavilion were dangerously eroded, the building did not collapse.

The storm ripped away a large chunk of the boardwalk and carried away much of Surf Avenue. The cottages that once lined the landward side of the avenue now teetered on the edge of a sandy precipice. In addition to battering the Delaware coast, the storm inflicted similar damage on seaside towns in New Jersey. At Seabright, the *New York Times* reported, "When it was seen that human opposition [to the storm] could do nothing to stop the destruction, women with their garments blown by the wind kneeled together in the street some distance from the ocean and prayed: 'Almighty God, quiet the sea, still the winds, and save our city.'"

The *Times* also reported, "The entire beach front of the Rehoboth, Del., resort is a wreck. More than 200 feet of the boardwalk was washed away, and other parts of it were damaged. Several buildings along the beach were undermined. At Dewey Beach, two miles below Rehoboth, a strip of land 1,000 feet wide between the bay and the ocean, is submerged." This would not be the last time that the narrow neck of land south of Dewey Beach would be flooded from the ocean to the coastal bay.

After the storm dissipated, Horn's Pavilion was torn down, and a more substantial building was constructed on the north side of Rehoboth Avenue. Several dozen cottages on Surf Avenue were also moved westward to be on more solid ground, and a new boardwalk was built. The people of Rehoboth were still in love with the sea, but they had a newfound respect for its fury.

Surf Avenue viewed from the south (Horn's Pavilion is on the right) after the 1914 storm. *Courtesy of the Rehoboth Historical Society.*

Viewed from the north, Horn's Pavilion is in the distance on the right. *Courtesy of the Rehoboth Historical Society.*

The 1914 storm undermined several oceanfront buildings. *Courtesy of the Rehoboth Historical Society.*

Cape Henlopen: Uprooted Trees and Beached Ships

In April 1918, the weather turned foul as the steam-tug *Eastern* plowed its way through a storm with two barges, the *Merrimac* and the *Severn*, in tow. The strong winds drove the steam-tug, the *Merrimac* and the *Severn* toward the shore in the vicinity of the recently rebuilt boardwalk. As the three vessels approached the beach, the crew of the *Eastern* cut the lines that bound the tug to the *Merrimac* and the *Severn*. Freed of the barges that were dragging it toward shore, the tug was able to power out to deeper water. The wind, however, continued to propel the *Merrimac* and the *Severn* toward the shore, and the two barges did not stop until they grounded on the beach in front of the demolished boardwalk, nearly on the doorstep of the houses that lined the oceanfront.

The 640-ton *Merrimac* had sustained significant damage, and the barge began to settle into the sand. The *Severn* was relatively unscathed as it slid to a stop, and after the storm subsided, tugs were able to float the *Severn* free. The *Merrimac*, however, was so deeply trapped in the sand that it was left to settle on the Rehoboth beach. The 1914 hurricane and 1918 nor'easter were typical in the way that they rearranged the dunes and drove ships onto the beach, but these storms happened to do this on the oceanfront

The *Merrimac* (*in the background*) on the beach at Rehoboth. *Courtesy of the Rehoboth Historical Society.*

The Cape Henlopen Lighthouse three months before it collapsed. *Courtesy of the Delaware Public Archives.*

at Rehoboth, where homes and hotels had been built on the sand, and vacationers frolicked on the beach.

North of Rehoboth, these two storms continued the erosion of the dune that supported the Cape Henlopen lighthouse. By the early 1920s, the beacon teetered on the edge of a sandy precipice with parts of the tower's foundation exposed. On March 21, 1926, Thomas Hill wrote in the *New York Times*:

> *Old Henlopen Light, which guards the Delaware Capes, was reported to Benjamin Franklin 137 years ago as in danger of being washed away. Today it is threatened again—so fiercely threatened that hope of saving it for longer service has almost been abandoned. After saving hundreds of vessels with its mighty rays and seeing many a good ship go to pieces on the perilous sands it seems to be doomed at last by the relentless sea.*

Several wooden groins had been constructed on the beach near the eroding dune that held the lighthouse in an effort to catch the sand that migrated along the coast, but these did little good. Hill reported that there were also plans to sink surplus ships from World War I in the vicinity of the lighthouse to create an artificial reef that would form "a buffer that will not only halt the erosion of the sand beneath the foundation of the light but will also create a current that will actually restore the sand already cut away." There was little hope that this plan would work. According to Hill, "army engineers place little faith in these plans. They say the protection will be temporary and must be put into effect quickly, for it will take only one or two more big nor'easters to end the career of the historic Henlopen beacon."

A month later, there was no nor'easter blowing on April 13, 1926, when yet another government committee studying how to save the lighthouse was enjoying lunch below deck on a small boat near the cape. One of the committeemen had remained on deck and was watching the lighthouse, which seemed to be leaning a little more than usual. Moments later, he interrupted the committee's lunch with a cry of, "It's gone!" The Cape Henlopen Lighthouse had tumbled onto the beach, victim of the moving sands of the Delmarva coast.

Immediately after the collapse of the tower, residents from Lewes and Rehoboth descended on the rubble to collect souvenirs from the fallen lighthouse. Preserved as revered relics of bygone days, some of these chunks of stone found their way to museums in Lewes and Rehoboth.

A scaled-down version of the Cape Henlopen Lighthouse greets visitors to the resort from a roundabout on Rehoboth Avenue. *Photo by Michael Morgan.*

While the people of Lewes mourned the loss of the lighthouse as they would the loss of an old friend, in Rehoboth, the memory of the lighthouse was kept alive by the construction of a replica of the old tower. Today, an impressive but scaled-down version of the Cape Henlopen Lighthouse greets visitors to the resort from a roundabout on Rehoboth Avenue as they enter the town.

CHAPTER 4

OCEAN CITY: 1933

TO TAKE THE SALT AIR

When the Vagabond Hurricane swept over Ocean City in 1903, the Maryland resort town was barely three decades old. In 1869, Isaac Coffin opened the Rhode Island Inn—for fishermen, hunters and other vacationers—on the Maryland beach, where a bulge in the mainland reduced the coastal bay to a relatively narrow channel. Tradition has it that Coffin fished a name board out of the surf with "Rhode Island" on it and so named his new hotel. Whether the ship that once carried the name board had succumbed to a storm is not known, but Coffin was not concerned about a hurricane or nor'easter damaging his new establishment. In a time when water transportation was common on the Delmarva Peninsula, visitors to Coffin's inn did not seem to mind the short boat ride across Sinepuxent Bay. In just a few years, the Rhode Island Inn was joined by other small hotels as developers saw the potential in the continuous ribbon of pristine Assateague sand, and the growing cluster of buildings on the Maryland coast soon became known as "Ocean City."

In 1875, the new Atlantic Hotel—with an excellent orchestra, a fine restaurant and an unobstructed view of the beach—opened with great fanfare; soon afterward, a railroad trestle was built across Sinepuxent Bay, and the train was able to roll directly into Ocean City. The Atlantic Hotel proved so popular that in five years it was expanded and became the signature hotel in the growing Maryland resort town. By the 1880s, the area on the Maryland coast boasted three large and excellent hotels, several boardinghouses, two churches, a number of private cottages and a lifesaving station. Wells driven to a depth of seventy-five to eighty feet produced clean, cold water. A principal reason that Ocean City blossomed was that the beach quickly gained a reputation for being one of the finest on the Atlantic coast. As was common in the resorts that sprang up on the Delmarva barrier islands, the owners of many early hotels at Ocean City ignored the fact that storm-driven waves often inundated the beach and drove the ocean water across the dunes. These hardheaded businessmen built their hotels on the very edge of the dunes to give their guests a good view of the surf and take full advantage of the ocean breezes.

The town leaders did not completely ignore the effects of storms. When the first Ocean City boardwalk (a prerequisite for a first-class seaside resort) was built in the space between the hotels and the surf, it was constructed in sections so that it could be taken up at the end of the summer and stored

Ocean City in the early twentieth century. *Courtesy of the Delaware Public Archives.*

to prevent damage from winter storms. Much of the early boardwalk was elevated, and it was high enough that a person could easily walk underneath it. Squeezed into the area between the buildings and the breakers at high tide, the ocean washed under the boards. Almost from the beginning, it was apparent that the sands of the part of the Maryland coast where Ocean City sat were migrating from north to south. In an effort to keep the wayward sand in place, rows of pilings were driven into the beach. Early visitors to Ocean City shared the unpaved, sandy streets with horses and oxen pulling carriages and carts. Also mingling with the bathers on the beach were the wild ponies of Assateague that roamed freely on the sand. Not only were ponies allowed to wander about the resort, but Ocean City did not ban hogs from traipsing around the town until 1915.

According to *A Paradise for Gunners and Anglers* (a guidebook for sportsmen published in 1883 by the Philadelphia, Wilmington & Baltimore Railroad Company), hunting and fishing in the immediate vicinity of Ocean City was exceptionally good. Fishing from the railroad bridge and in the channels of the coastal bays, anglers caught perch, striped bass, sea bass and spot, and hunters found wildfowl and shore birds plentiful in their seasons.

At the south edge of the resort was a camp for fishermen that was unique among the Delmarva resorts. In the late nineteenth century, Christopher Ludlam arrived in Ocean City. A veteran of the U.S. Life-Saving Service, Ludlam understood the coastal waters and the fish that swam in them better than most people. Ignoring the menhaden that inhabited the deep ocean waters, Ludlam sought the schools of edible and profitable trout and bluefish that migrated along the beach a short distance from the surf. The resort's railroad trestle across Sinepuxent Bay brought vacationers into the resort, and he believed that he could use the same train facilities to ship tons of fish to Philadelphia, Baltimore and other cities. The only problem was that there was no inlet across Assateague Island in the vicinity of Ocean City, and the only way of reaching the fish was to launch a boat through the surf.

Ludlam's experience in the Life-Saving Service taught him that on clear, sunny days that were ideal for vacationing beachgoers, a storm in the distant Atlantic could churn up the sea and send high surf thundering ashore on the Delmarva coast. During Ludlam's years in the Life-Saving Service, he was well drilled in how to launch a surfboat through the breakers. He knew how to look for the right waves to initiate the drive through the surf, how to keep the boat at a right angle to the waves and how the fishermen had to pull on the oars in unison. One mistake could overturn the boat, and if the fishermen were returning to shore with a boat loaded with the day's catch, the risk was even greater. A misjudged wave could upset the fish-laden boat and dump several hours of hard work back into the sea. Undeterred by these difficulties, Ludlam built a fish pound a short distance from the beach. A series of pilings were driven into the ocean floor, and these posts were used to string a system of nets that funneled the fish into a large holding area. After the fish had been collected in the pound, the fishermen launched their boats and began pulling the catch aboard, spilling the wiggling fish into the bottom of the open boat.

With the catch safely aboard, the fishermen would guide the boat to shore for the ride through the plunging surf. After the boat had slid onto the sand, horses were used to pull the boat, heavy with fish, over a series of rollers laid on the sand.

Most of the fish were sorted, iced and loaded onto the train, but some of the catch was delivered to Ocean City restaurants and local residents. Spurred by Ludlam's success, a dozen pound-fishing enterprises operated from the beach at the south end of town and provided a diversion for sightseeing vacationers. The pound-fishing season ran from spring through the fall, and the industry was so successful that it employed three-quarters of the men working in Ocean City.

In 1933, Ocean City was over fifty years old, and cars had replaced the train as the principal mode of transportation to reach the resort. The pound fishermen still launched their boats through the surf, and some even took vacationers through the breakers and into the Atlantic so that they could experience deep-sea fishing. After storms and the slow migration of sand had closed all of the natural inlets that had once crossed Assateague, the town leaders of Ocean City longed for a waterway from the Atlantic to the coastal bays that would provide a calm harbor for fishing boats. An attempt to dig an inlet before World War I ended in failure when the shallow waterway quickly silted closed. Similar efforts (some using explosives to blast a waterway across the sand) to deepen and widen the Indian River Inlet in Delaware ended with the same result. The relentless movement of the sand filled whatever watery channels were created. Following World War I, the state of Maryland appropriated $500,000 to cover two-thirds of the cost of digging a new inlet, and the leaders of Ocean City lobbied the federal government for the rest of the funds to construct a new waterway. With the election of President Franklin Roosevelt and the coming of the New Deal, it appeared that funds might be available, but in early 1933, Congress postponed consideration of a bill to construct the inlet.

Ocean City: 1933

Poles used by pound fishermen on the Ocean City beach. *Courtesy of the Julia A. Purnell Museum.*

Pound fishermen at work. *Courtesy of the Julia A. Purnell Museum.*

Although Ocean City was Maryland's only Atlantic resort and one of the major vacation destinations on the Delmarva coast, some people preferred the calmer waters of the coastal bays. Public Landing, on the western shore of Chincoteague Bay due east of Snow Hill, had been welcoming visitors before Ocean City was established. Vacationers at Public Landing and Ocean City enjoyed picnicking, crabbing and boating on the waters of the coastal bays. Both resorts had boardwalks, piers, dance halls, merry-go-rounds and other amusements. Public Landing, however, did not have the ocean surf, the pound fishermen or the Assateague ponies. Although it was several miles from the coast, Public Landing would not be immune to the storms that periodically swept along the Delmarva coast.

ASSATEAGUE: PARADISE FOR SPORTSMEN

As Ocean City grew, south of the resort, Assateague remained mostly undeveloped by humans, but Mother Nature continued to reshape the coast by periodically opening and closing the inlets that led to the coastal bays. When Verrazano arrived in 1524, the Italian explorer picked his way through the winding waterway that separated Chincoteague Island from Assateague. Known as Chincoteague Inlet, this meandering channel did not cross the beach directly from the ocean to the coastal bay but instead looped around the southern tip of Assateague. Verrazano was fortunate that he was able to navigate without much difficulty. During colonial times, other sailing-ship captains found Chincoteague Inlet a nightmare to navigate. Some very patient captains waited several weeks before winds and tides combined to allow them to safely sail through the inlet.

If Chincoteague Inlet had one redeeming asset, it was that it remained open throughout the last several hundred years. The need to cross the waterway for access discouraged development on Assateague, but a substantial village arose on Chincoteague Island, and by the late nineteenth century, it was a thriving town of about 2,500 residents. According to *A Paradise for Gunners and Anglers*, "The hotel accommodations [at Chincoteague] are excellent at two dollars per day; and, as almost the entire population is constantly engaged either in oystering, fishing, or gunning, there is little difficulty in finding boats and boatmen for all kinds of sport, at moderate rates."

North of Chincoteague, there were several inlets that crossed Assateague at various times. Some of these waterways lasted only a few years, and in the cases of inlets opened by strong storms, they were closed in a matter of months. In an 1837 report to Maryland governor Thomas Ward Veazey, John H. Alexander, the first state geologist for Maryland, provided a summary of the inlets that once crossed Assateague. At the time of his report, the Maryland coast was one continuous ribbon of sandy beach. There were no open inlets between Indian River Inlet in Delaware to the north and Chincoteague Inlet in Virginia to the south, a distance of nearly fifty miles. Writing in 1837, Alexander noted that the Maryland coast:

> *is protected by a beach, consisting originally (by that is meant, hardly 100 years ago) of a number of small islands…At present that original arrangement is broken up to a certain degree by the junction into one of all the islands and their connect with the mainland at the northern end, so that in fact from Indian river inlet down to Chincoteague the beach is a long peninsula of 50 miles, varying in width from one hundred yards to nearly a mile.*

Alexander went on to explain that the terminology of this part of the coast derived from the time when some of the inlets were still in existence and broke Assateague into various segments:

> *The ancient names, which were attributed to the different islands when they were islands, are still in good many places retained for different portions of the peninsula. Thus we have, Assateague Island, now the southernmost extremity of the peninsula; Sinepuxent, against Sinepuxent Neck, and joining on to Assateague—the Rocking Islands, the Middle Pines, Fenwick's Island, and others whose names will occur to those familiar with those localities.*

With the Maryland coastal bays locked behind the barrier island, Alexander suggested the construction of an inlet opposite the mouth of Saint Martin's River to facilitate trade by farmers in that area. He dismissed the value of Indian River Inlet in Delaware, explaining that it was rarely six feet deep at high tide and about three feet deep when the tide ebbed. Alexander believed that this inlet would likely close at any time and that a new inlet might replace it farther north on Rehoboth Bay.

The most important inlet in colonial times was the Sinepuxent Inlet that crossed Assateague about ten miles south of Ocean City. In 1698, several justices of the peace for Sussex County, Delaware, wrote to the colonial

Fiesta Park, in north Ocean City, retains some of the woods that once were common on Fenwick Island. *Photo by Michael Morgan.*

authorities that pirates had captured a sloop belonging to a Philadelphia merchant as it was "coming out of Cinnepuxon Inlett." The pirates sailed northward along the Delmarva coast until they rounded Cape Henlopen and reached Lewes, where they "landed about 50 men, well armed and came up ye town and plundered almost every house…breaking open doors and chests, and taking away all money or plate to be found…together with rugs, blanketing and all other bed covering, leaving scare anything in ye place to cover or wear."

Sinepuxent Inlet continued to be an important waterway throughout colonial times; the area on the north side of the channel became known as "North Beach," and the corresponding area on the south side was known as "South Beach." During the American Revolution, Sinepuxent Inlet was so important that the colonists fortified it to prevent its use by the British. In March 1777, the American privateer *General Mifflin*, commanded by a Captain Hamilton, was sailing along the coast when it was overtaken by a storm. Hamilton decided to run into Sinepuxent Inlet and ride out the storm, but he ran into a sandbar with such force that it knocked a hole in the hull of the *General Mifflin*. The ship soon filled with water, and according to the *Pennsylvania Gazette*, "The hands (ninety odd) were on the quarter deck the whole night, and suffered exceedingly and in the morning go on shore on a desolate beach, covered with snow where seventeen perished." The other crewmen were saved, but the *General Mifflin*, along with three thousand pounds worth of captured goods, were lost. By the end of the Revolution, however, sand—which, on this part of the Maryland coast, migrates from north to south—had begun to cover the remains of the *General Mifflin* and accumulate in the inlet. By the early nineteenth century, Sinepuxent Inlet had permanently silted shut.

Most of the other inlets across Assateague Island existed for such a short time that they did not acquire names. In 1920, a storm created an inlet three or four miles south of Ocean City, but in 1928, a nor'easter filled the unnamed inlet with sand. One of the temporary waterways that lasted long enough to be named was Green Run Inlet, which cut across Assateague Island about four miles north of the Virginia line. It appears that this inlet was opened by the natural movement of the sand in the middle of the nineteenth century and lasted for about thirty years. The channel was deep and wide enough for small boats to navigate through it, but a sandbar on the bayside of the inlet made it useless for commercial vessels. A small beach village developed at Green Run, and in the early 1880s, there was a summer hotel, Scott's Ocean House, and a Life-Saving Service station. However, because it was difficult to access, the settlement at Green Run withered away.

Even when the inlets existed, most were shallow, fordable waterways that wildlife could cross without much difficulty. White-tailed deer, sika deer (introduced during the 1920s), foxes, raccoons, Delmarva fox squirrels and others thrive on Assateague. There was reason to believe that wolves once roamed the island. Early visitors to Assateague were attracted by the numerous species of wildlife. According to *A Paradise for Gunners and Anglers*,

> *On the Atlantic shores, the choicest game birds in the world are found, and in such quantity, in their respective season, that the gunner is afforded almost constant opportunity for the exercise of his skill. It would be difficult to find, anywhere, a territory of the same extent, frequented by such large variety and immense numbers of fish and game. This abundance is not confined to a few localities, but is distributed through nearly every part.*

Anglers also found good fishing in the coastal waters:

> *Go where you will in the appropriate season, whether "outside" on the ocean, where the bluefish is the autocrat, in the surf among the breakers, where the drum forages, or in the bays, inlets, sounds, few-water rivers, creeks or ponds, where finny game in endless variety have their habitats, and you have but to drop a baited hook to secure a quick response from beneath the waters—a response that not infrequently takes either your breath or your hook.*

Unlike Rehoboth in Delaware and Ocean City in Maryland, Assateague had no boardwalk, carousel, bowling alleys or other amusements. It did, however, have the ever-present ponies and the Atlantic Ocean, which travel writer Bayard Taylor described as "growing gray in the sunset," breaking in long, lazy swells where bathers met "the great, lifting masses of water, and rode them as if they were tame elephants."

The beauty of Assateague south of Ocean City was the unbroken line of beach so that a horse and carriage could drive southward from the resort for a distance of approximately forty miles. Along the way, the riders could see gulls skimming over the surf, hawks hunting prey in the dunes and ducks and geese and the occasional whales and other large sea creatures in the ocean. Never more than a half-mile wide, Assateague was sometimes pinched by the coastal bay and the ocean to a width of just a few hundred feet. The bay on the west side of Assateague was ten miles wide in some places and narrowed to two hundred yards in others. Ranging from two to five feet deep, it was the home of first-rate oysters. It was not unusual to see the broad expanse of the bay covered with wild fowl, including mallards, canvasbacks, black ducks, brants and teals in flocks as thick as those of the wildebeest in the Serengeti.

The sportsmen who hunted for wildfowl along the Delmarva coast endured harsh conditions in the quest for their prey. After rising in the middle of the night, the hunters trekked across the dunes to a suitable location near the coastal bay frequented by the wildfowl. Some gunners dug holes in the sand; others hid behind a blind, standing waist-deep in water. In either case, a string of decoys was deployed to entice the passing birds to come within range.

A successful hunt often meant suffering attacks by mosquitoes, sand flies and other pesky residents of the coast. In addition, the gentlemen sportsmen sometimes endured hours half-submerged in bone-chilling water. After the day's hunt was completed, the game was gathered together, and the sportsmen retraced their steps to their modest accommodations, where they

Ocean City: 1933

The remains of a wooden shipwreck on Assateague Island. *Photo by Michael Morgan.*

spent the evening in the common sitting room smoking pipes and discussing guns, decoys and the habits of various birds.

After storms, the hunters and fishermen were joined by people from the mainland eager to locate ships that had been driven on to the beach. If the storm deposited the hull so high on the Assateague beach that it was impossible to refloat, everything of value was stripped from the vessel and carted off. Sometimes, this salvaging was done by the owners of the stranded ship; often, however, the foundered vessel was stripped by swarms of beachcombers from the mainland who descended upon any ship unlucky enough to be driven ashore. In either case, the lower hull was left behind, and the abandoned timbers were soon covered by the shifting sands.

Most of the hulks buried along the Assateague coast have little historical value, but the discovery of the timbers of an old wreck after a passing storm conjures up images of pirate ships and their chests of ill-gotten treasure. So far as is known, no buccaneer booty has been discovered on Assateague, but in addition to the timbers of old ships, the shifting sands sometimes reveal the stumps of ancient trees that were part of the cedar and pine forests that once lined the coast. The remains of these trees are chilling reminders that the Delmarva barrier islands are migrating westward.

AN INLET WAS BORN

The storm that would dramatically change the Delmarva coast was born over nine hundred miles east of Puerto Rico on Wednesday, August 16, 1933, when a steamship, the *Western Prince*, reported winds of over forty miles per hour and a heavy southeast swell. For two days, the storm moved westward until it took a more northerly track that carried it to about 150 miles southwest of Bermuda. The next day, the storm changed course to the west and began to bear down on the mid-Atlantic coast. On Monday morning, August 21, storm warnings were posted from Cape Hatteras and Boston advising the approach of a strong tropical system. At 4:00 p.m. the next day, the U.S. Weather Bureau issued the following statement: "Atlantic coast disturbances central about 150 miles southeast of Cape Hatteras, moving slightly north of west. Center will cross southern coast of North Carolina early Wednesday forenoon, preceded by dangerous shifting gales tonight between Virginia Capes and Southport, N.C. Advise all interests."

Along the Delmarva coast, the storm-generated rain had begun falling on Friday, while the storm was still several hundred miles from Ocean City. As the rain continued in torrents over the weekend, vacationers expecting a late summer day on a sunny beach began to pack up and head for home. Although the center of the storm would pass one hundred miles from the Delmarva coast, its northeast winds battered the coast for several days, eroding the dunes and flooding the coastal bays. Having brushed Cape Hatteras, the storm passed over Norfolk, Virginia, and continued up the west side of the Chesapeake Bay to Washington, D.C. Hidden by the storm clouds, the moon was full and generating abnormally high tides as the hurricane drenched the Delmarva coast. At Chincoteague and other communities on Virginia's Eastern Shore, gales between fifty and eighty miles per hour drove the ocean waters over the beaches and marshes into the mainland. Ocean breakers reached as far as Chincoteague and flooded the streets.

In Ocean City, the prodigiously large amount of water dumped on the resort by the storm was having a telling effect. When it became apparent that the storm would have a devastating effect on the resort, the few vacationers fled in panic, leaving behind their luggage with some people wearing only bathing suits. South of town, shacks, poles and nets for the fish pounds were washed out to sea. A large cement septic tank used by the fishermen was rolled across the beach and out to sea. In town, the boardwalk began to give way, splintering into thousands of pieces and leaving a forest of support

OCEAN CITY: 1933

Laurel, an inland community, was flooded by the 1933 hurricane. *Courtesy of the Delaware Public Archives.*

pilings behind. Water flooded the streets and lower floors of buildings. When the railroad trestle gave way and the causeway into town was damaged, there was no way out of the resort. Those who had not evacuated were left to hunker down and wait for the wind and water to recede.

As the bay waters behind Ocean City continued to rise, farther up the coast, Bethany Beach and Rehoboth were being battered. According to the *Delaware Coast News*:

> *About 100 feet of the Boardwalk between Brooklyn and Delaware Avenues in Rehoboth was washed away. A section of the boardwalk in front of the Ewing Construction Company building was damaged. Silver Lake overflowed and the water coming in from the Ocean flowed into the streets and flooded the cellars of the properties on Queen Street and lakeside Drive. The piers belonging to Mrs. Waterman and Mr. Charles Watson were washed away.*

Fifteen-foot waves broke over the boardwalk near the Henlopen Hotel, and the water raced down Lake Avenue toward Lake Gerar. On Rehoboth Avenue, a number of young trees that had been planted during a mosquito eradication program were uprooted. These trees were so small that when they fell, they did not damage any of the nearby buildings. Other than a few signs being blown down, none of the structures in Rehoboth were damaged, and no one was injured in the storm. On the bayside of Cape Henlopen, Lewes Beach was flooded, and the road from the beach to town was underwater. Several barges and boats rode out the storm in the relativity safe waters behind the breakwater, but the high water lifted two small yachts onto the beach. The fish plant piers escaped the storm undamaged.

While most attention was focused on the damage that was being done by the wind and waves along the oceanfront, the constant rain continued to fill the coastal bays. In Rehoboth, Silver Lake threatened to overflow its banks and flood nearby houses. A group of firemen attempted to cut an opening from the lake to the ocean, but they were unsuccessful. At Ocean City, however, it was a different story. The surf continued to hammer away at the sand, eroding the beach westward. At the same time, the rain continued to fill the coastal bays to overflowing. As with any container filled with water, the liquid pushes against the side of the vessel as it seeks a weak spot to escape. The water level on Assawoman, Isle of Wight and Sinepuxent Bays was now higher than the ocean, and the accumulated water pushed against the banks of the bays, striving for some way to relieve the pressure. Finally, the sand gave way. A short distance from South Division Street in the vicinity of the fish camps, the bay waters pushed through the barrier island and drove the retreating sand into the ocean. The water from the coastal bays rushed through the new channel, eroding the sides and bottom of the new waterway and making it wider and deeper. The storm had given Ocean City its long-sought inlet!

As the hurricane continued northward and the rain and wind subsided in Ocean City, the Coast Guard used one of its small boats to navigate the resort's water-filled streets and rescue several people in flooded buildings. Debris from the boardwalk and buildings was everywhere, and in the ensuing weeks, the boardwalk would be rebuilt and buildings repaired so that Ocean City could be open for business when the first summer vacationers arrived the next year. It was not, however, business as usual. The water in the new inlet continued its steady flow from the coastal bays into the ocean for another five days. The resort's town leaders and state officials quickly secured funding to stabilize the new inlet to make it a permanent feature

Ocean City: 1933

The Ocean City Inlet provides a direct waterway from the ocean to the inland bays. *Photo by Michael Morgan.*

of the Delmarva coast. The pound fishermen were replaced by commercial and recreational fishermen whose boats sailed out of the harbors on the calm waters of the coastal bay through the inlet.

Toward the north in Rehoboth, the Delaware resort's residents also went to work to clean up the debris and return the town to normal. Some proclaimed it the worst storm to hit Rehoboth since the 1914 storm that forced one hundred cottage owners to move their houses back from the beach. A few days later, however, the *New York Times* reported: "Rehoboth Beach, Del., a fishing center and summer resort, was reported literally washed into the sea." Wilbur Corkran, a veteran of World War I, the developer of Henlopen Acres and one of the town's staunchest supporters, was not a man who backed off from a fight. Corkran dashed off a letter to the editor of the *Times* that pointed out that Rehoboth residents and resort visitors "enjoyed the storm to the fullest extent and crowded down to the sea front to see the waves dash onto the beach." Rehoboth, Corkran wrote, "was neither washed out to sea nor seriously damaged."

The hurricane had been featured on the front page of the *New York Times*, which devoted several stories and pictures to the storm. Corkran's rebuttal of this coverage was published a week later among the letters to the editor, and Corkran was convinced that he had set the record straight. Other supporters of Rehoboth took a less serious approach to the *Times* report of the town being "wiped out by the storm," which was repeated by several other newspapers. A week after the storm, the *Delaware Coast News* published an account by "E.G.," who claimed to be "one of the several sole survivors" of the hurricane. Although some oceanfront resorts had sustained considerable damage, in Rehoboth, according to E.G., "The waves did roll; reached clear to the dunes, and there deposited enough of the boardwalks and buildings of Cape May, Ocean City and other resorts to supply us diligent beachcombers with firewood sufficient for the winter."

In Rehoboth, E.G. maintained, "A few screens were blown in on the porches of the water front cottages" and Rehoboth's residents were blasé about the storm; "I must admit that while the rain was on, the whole town was dampish, but when that stopped everyone went out to see the show, enjoy the sunshine and cuss because the American Store had no bread (because the bakers in the city were all washed up)." The rain dumped a great deal of water on the coast, and

> *the Bay got a little larger than usual, thus giving the tame geese a wider swimming pool, but there were no mosquitoes. Both lakes in town were full of water—and a good lake is one of the best places for water I know of. Fishing was one from both front and back porches of the Carpenter cottage; Governor* [C. Douglass] *Buck was sitting pretty in the Cannon place with this end of the State under complete control but the northern counties missing.*

E.G. saw some of the damage as being an improvement, "In front of the Henlopen Hotel the boardwalk was bulged a bit. For three years to my knowledge the customers have complained to the management that there were no good spitting cracks. They are now satisfied and everyone is delighted with its present condition." In addition, he maintained, "A great quantity of dirty sand and broken glass was washed off the beach, and a greater quantity of clean sand washed in so that at present this undoubtedly the finest beach on the eastern coast." E.G.'s sarcastic letter concluded that, far from being destroyed by the storm and washed into the sea, Rehoboth "is still here, even to the Tourist Camp [in the grove on the west end of town]."

After the storm subsided, firemen succeeded in opening a small channel from Silver Lake to the ocean to allow the excess water to drain into the

Ocean City: 1933

Atlantic. Unlike at Ocean City, where the waterway between the ocean and the coastal bay became permanent, Rehoboth's new inlet was quickly closed. Along the Delmarva coast, the 1933 storm overwashed the beach and created a number of shallow, temporary inlets. In Ocean City, there was little development north of Seventeenth Street, and the several breaches in the dunes that created momentary channels between the ocean and the coastal bays went mostly unnoticed. The conditions that created these small, transitory inlets would remain in place as Ocean City began to expand up the coast to the Delaware line over the next couple of decades.

CHAPTER 5
Nature Takes Its Toll

GREAT ATLANTIC HURRICANE: 1944

As communities along the Delmarva coast recovered from the 1933 storm, the growing popularity of the automobile continued to affect the landscape of the coastal region. Gone were the passenger trains that once brought the majority of vacationers to Rehoboth and Ocean City. In their place were swarms of cars jamming the roads that led to the coast. The increased traffic prompted government officials from Delaware and Maryland to plan an improved coastal highway that would run from Ocean City to Rehoboth Beach. The project would include a new bridge over the newly dredged Indian River Inlet, which had been stabilized by the construction of stone groins on either side of the waterway.

As work on the coastal road inched its way to completion, the *Delaware Coast News* proclaimed the Delaware coast to be "a real American Riviera" and anticipated increased development of Rehoboth, Dewey Beach, Bethany and Fenwick Island. At the same time, Ocean City, Maryland, hemmed in from expanding southward by the new inlet, began its relentless march northward toward Delaware. After the hard-surfaced road that had been completed in 1937 made the beaches on Cape Henlopen more accessible, hundreds of thousands of tourists from all over the United States visited the cape to fish in the surf, climb the steep slopes of the famous Great Dune, eat picnic lunches on the wide beaches and camp among the scrub pine–dotted dunes.

Nature Takes Its Toll

Rehoboth during the 1930s. *Courtesy of the Rehoboth Historical Society.*

At ten in the morning on Monday, December 9, 1940, a year before the Japanese attack on Pearl Harbor, a three-plane squad of two-seater A-T-6 advance trainers, temporarily based at Rehoboth airfield, took off to attack Cape Henlopen's Great Dune. After climbing to five thousand feet, the aircraft descended to five hundred feet and opened fire on three ten-by-six-foot metal targets nestled in the sand. The squadron of trainers strafed the targets with machine fire, then circled for another attack on the motionless targets. For the next two months, the attacks on the cape became a twice-daily occurrence, disrupting the sand and tearing up vegetation. The damage to the Great Dune was less than that caused by the annual Easter egg roll when kids chased eggs down the edge of the Great Dune and older folks—more adventurous but no more mature—ran their cars up the side of the dune in a show of mechanical masculinity. The ridge of sand barely had time to recover before the cape was invaded by an army of workers who would permanently alter the dunes along the Delaware coast.

A restored gun battery at Fort Miles. *Photo by Michael Morgan.*

After World War II began in Europe, the federal government purchased over one thousand acres of land on Cape Henlopen, including the Great Dune, for the construction of a modern military installation. A 3,500-foot-long railroad was built across the marshes, and two and a half miles of heavy-duty highway were constructed from Lewes to the cape to carry the heavy construction and military equipment that was needed for the vast military complex. Toolsheds sprang up among the scrub pines in preparation for the start of construction, and piles for an 1,800-foot-long government pier were driven in the bay bottom near the site of the old "Iron Pier" (built in the late nineteenth century but never quite completed), although it had been used for half a century. Finally, the sand was deeply scarred with trenches to carry water pipes and electric lines to the new facility.

When the facility became fully operational during World War II, the cape was strewn with major gun batteries, artillery emplacements and an assortment of barracks and other support buildings. The major changes in the landscape of the cape came from the construction of below-ground batteries, some of which housed enormous sixteen-inch guns capable of firing a one-ton shell over twenty miles. A series of concrete towers were to

Nature Takes Its Toll

A four-hundred-foot corridor in an underground battery at Fort Miles. *Photo by Michael Morgan.*

be built along the beach. Like the fallen Cape Henlopen Lighthouse, these towers served as landmarks to measure the westward migration of the coast. The new facility on Cape Henlopen was named "Fort Miles" in honor of Nelson A. Miles, a prominent Civil War general.

Fort Miles was quiet in September 1944, when what became known as the "Great Atlantic Hurricane" came roaring up the Delmarva coast. After pounding the beaches at Assateague, the storm did minimal damage to Ocean City. In Delaware, the nescient community at Fenwick Island flooded; and at Bethany Beach, the boardwalk was torn up, and the flood waters carried debris into the streets.

In 1923, four brothers—Ross, Harry, Walter and Raymond Ringler—had opened a theater on the boardwalk near Garfield Avenue in Bethany Beach. The Ringler brothers showed silent movies, which were accompanied by the lively sounds of a piano. On Saturday nights, the folding chairs used by the movie patrons were cleared away to create a dance floor, and with music provided by local bands, the Ringler Theater became one of the most popular date spots on the coast. But, the wooden building on the boardwalk could not withstand the ocean waves and was reduced to a loose stack of debris by the 1944 hurricane.

Above: Some of the remaining above-ground buildings at Fort Miles. *Photo by Michael Morgan.*

Left: One of the dozen observation towers that provided support for the large guns at Fort Miles. *Photo by Michael Morgan.*

NATURE TAKES ITS TOLL

The Great Atlantic Hurricane of 1944 flooded Bethany Beach. *Courtesy of the Delaware Public Archives.*

The Seaside Inn, a Bethany landmark, surrounded by sand after the 1944 storm. *Courtesy of the Delaware Public Archives.*

In Bethany, the 1944 storm destroyed the boardwalk. The stock of debris to the left of the surviving buildings was once the Ringler Theater. *Courtesy of the Delaware Public Archives.*

The 1944 storm carried sand and debris into the streets of Bethany Beach. *Courtesy of the Delaware Public Archives.*

Nature Takes Its Toll

North of Bethany, the high wind and water of the hurricane flooded across the dunes, inundated the coastal highway, uprooted trees, destroyed utility poles, ripped boats from their moorings and sank a barge in the Lewes-Rehoboth Canal.

Off Cape Henlopen, the captain of the 254-foot-long tanker *Thomas Tracy* struggled to maintain headway when the tanker's engines failed. The tanker was driven southward to almost the center of Rehoboth Beach, where the northeast winds drove the drifting ship onto the sand at the foot of Brooklyn Avenue.

With a telltale crack running up its side, the beached tanker settled into the sands of Rehoboth Beach, and when the storm cleared, sightseers poured into Rehoboth to see the startling sight of the ship resting on the sand. The tanker had come to rest over the timbers of the *Merrimac* that had been driven onto the beach in 1918. It was obvious from the large crack running up the side of the grounded tanker that the ship could not be refloated, and salvagers cut the hull into chunks to be trucked away. The lower parts of the ship were too difficult to salvage, and these were left behind.

The *Thomas Tracy* aground on the beach at Rehoboth. *Courtesy of the Delaware Public Archives.*

The *Thomas Tracy* on the sand at Rehoboth. *Courtesy of the Delaware Public Archives.*

At the end of World War II, the oceanside communities along the Delmarva coast resumed their normal summer schedules, but the coast was permanently changed. Vacationers got used to the Fort Miles spotting towers, but they were mostly unaware of the large bunkers hidden in the dunes and fragments of the *Thomas Tracy* buried in the Rehoboth sand.

BLUSTERY LADIES

Colonel Joe Duckworth was far from the Delmarva coast when he lost his cool. In the middle of World War II, Duckworth was stationed at Bryan Army Air Field, north of Houston, Texas, where he taught pilots the intricacies of instrument flying. The instrument-training school was unique, and British pilots, many of whom had done battle with Hitler's Luftwaffe, were flown to Bryan Field to learn how to fly using instruments. As the lead instructor, Duckworth's job was to teach them, but on July 27, 1943, he had had enough.

That morning, the weather forecast predicted that a hurricane would come ashore near Galveston, Texas, spread over Houston and inundate Bryan Field; many of the planes had to be flown to airfields out of the path of the storm. Some of the planes were AT-6 Texan Trainers, which were designed to be transition planes between a basic trainer and a front-line fighting aircraft. Some of the veteran British pilots considered it a step down to be flying the Texan Trainer rather than in a top-notch battle fighter. While the pilots were at breakfast, the news that the trainer aircraft would be flown away from the storm for safekeeping elicited some smiles and a few giggles from the hard-nosed British aviators, who began ribbing their American instructors about the fragile nature of the Texan Trainer. Finally, Duckworth shot back. He wagered a round of drinks that he could fly the Texan into the oncoming hurricane using only instruments and prove the stability of the aircraft along with the value of flying by instruments.

Colonel Duckworth recruited Lieutenant Ralph O'Hair, the only navigator available that morning, to fly with him. If their single engine was flooded by the driving rain and stalled, the two pilots would have the unique experience of parachuting into the full fury of a hurricane. Nevertheless, without official clearance, the two men flew off to hunt for the hurricane, which was not difficult to find. As they approached the storm at between four thousand and nine thousand feet, the turbulent air buffeted the small aircraft, and O'Hair said it was like "being tossed about like a stick in a dog's mouth." Undaunted, Duckworth and O'Hair continued to fly through the heavy rain and darkness as they navigated the strong, shifting winds.

Suddenly, all was calm and bright as they entered the eye of the storm. The small plane was surrounded by a ten-mile-diameter ring of black clouds that were dumping rain on to the Texas countryside. As the hurricane moved inland, the drag on the lower section of the storm seemed to tilt the eye forward. After the two flyers circled the eye, they plunged back into the heavy rain and winds to make their way back to Bryan Field. Weather officer Lieutenant William Jones-Burdick had learned what Duckworth and O'Hair were up to, and when they landed, he immediately asked to be flown into the storm. O'Hair quickly gave his seat to Jones-Burdick, and Duckworth took off again with the weather officer, who was eager to observe a hurricane from the inside. Duckworth's impromptu flights demonstrated that flying into a hurricane was not necessarily a recipe for disaster. The U.S. Weather Bureau then established a system of hurricane hunters who actively sought tropical systems before they hit the American coast. Responding to reports from ships at sea and other meteorological information, hurricane hunters would locate and fly into storms. As they crisscrossed the tropical system, those aboard the planes took measurements to determine the strength and direction of the storms. With this information, the U.S. Weather Bureau could alert coastal communities of the approach of a hurricane, and by the 1950s, storms could no longer sneak up on the Delmarva coast like the Vagabond Hurricane of 1903 did.

Strong and destructive storms usually acquired nicknames, like the Great Atlantic Hurricane of 1944. These names were haphazardly applied and sometimes misleading, as with the Great White Hurricane of 1888, which was a nor'easter and not a hurricane. The meteorologists used latitude and longitude to describe storms, and although this system was scientifically precise, it was clumsy for laypeople who needed to know of approaching storms. In 1950, the U.S. National Hurricane Center began naming Atlantic hurricanes according to the common phonetic alphabet (Able, Baker, Charlie, etc.). Each year, the first storm was named Able, the second Baker, and so forth. Although this was a simple and easy-to-remember system for the current year, the names were reused each year, so when looking back to compare storms, it quickly became apparent that, over time, it would be difficult to determine which "Able" storm was being referenced. To correct this problem, a system of unique names was instituted in 1953. Each year, an alphabetical list of female names was published to be applied to hurricanes. The names of hurricanes that caused widespread destruction were retired and replaced, and in 1979, the system began to use both male and female names.

It was not long after the National Hurricane Center began to apply female names to hurricanes that the Delmarva coast was visited by several blustery ladies. In 1950, Hurricane Carol formed in the Bahamas and moved northward, nipping past Cape Hatteras before moving parallel to the Delmarva coast. Four years later, Hurricane Hazel, a strong Category 4 storm, formed deeper in the West Indies, crossed the Bahamas and made landfall just north of Myrtle Beach, South Carolina. Continuing inland west of the Delmarva peninsula, Hazel pounded the coastal region with twenty-foot waves and strong winds. At Rehoboth, the storm was considered the worst since the Great Atlantic Hurricane of 1944, which drove the *Thomas Tracy* ashore. In 1955, Hurricane Connie followed a similar path and created higher-than-normal tides but caused minimal damage. The next year, however, Hurricane Flossy pounded the coast on September 28 and 29, and the ocean flowed over the dunes and flooded the road between Dewey and Bethany and damaged the beaches from Dewey to Fenwick Island. At Rehoboth, the storm eroded thousands of tons of sand from the beach; at high tide, the waves were breaking over the boardwalk but did no serious damage. In 1960, Hurricane Donna, packing 110-mph winds, damaged some beach cottages at Lewes, battered the Rehoboth boardwalk and breached the dunes between Indian River Inlet and Bethany Beach. The blustery ladies were an indication that storms were constantly reshaping the coast when, in October 1961, an unnamed nor'easter submerged two-thirds of the road between Dewey Beach and Fenwick Island under several feet of water. Bethany Beach and Lewes Beach were flooded, making streets impassible in those areas. The coast from Cape Henlopen to Assateague was severely eroded, but the damage was small compared to what was caused by another nor'easter that would strike six months later.

CHAPTER 6

Ash Wednesday Nor'easter: 1962

REALIZATION OF A DREAM

The storms of the 1950s did little to dissuade development along the Delmarva coast. From the time that the first vacationers from Washington and Baltimore arrived in Rehoboth and Ocean City, the Chesapeake Bay prevented easy access to the oceanfront resorts. After good railroad lines were completed to the coastal communities, it was possible to take a train up and around the Chesapeake Bay and down Delmarva to Rehoboth and Ocean City. Some vacationers opted to take a ferry from Baltimore to the Eastern Shore, where a railroad would whisk them to the coast. In the nineteenth century, when many vacationers stayed for the entire summer season, these travel arrangements were not difficult to accept. In the early twentieth century, however, horseless carriages began to rumble across Delmarva's roads, and an increasingly large number of people wanted to drive to the beach. Following World War I, improved roads and cars replaced passenger trains as the preferred mode of travel to the ocean resorts, and the Chesapeake Bay became more of a barrier to reaching the coast.

In 1938, the Ritchie Highway was completed, enabling Baltimore vacationers to reach the ferry landing near Annapolis with relative ease. The ferry took only forty-five minutes to cross the Chesapeake, but additional time was spent loading and unloading the cars, so using the ferry added as many as four hours to a trip to the coast. Resort visitors, politicians and others immediately began to agitate for a bridge across the Chesapeake Bay.

Ash Wednesday Nor'easter: 1962

After delays caused by World War II, opposition from Delmarva residents who feared an influx of motorists and concerns about creating a hazard to navigation on the bay, work began on the Chesapeake Bay Bridge in 1949, and three years later, the bridge was ready to open. On July 30, 1952, Maryland governor Theodore R. McKeldin led the first cars across the new bridge, marking the realization of a dream for those who wanted a quick and comfortable way to reach the oceanfront resorts in a matter of a few hours without getting out of their cars.

Almost immediately, vacationers began to flood into Ocean City, much to the delight of developers like Richard Hall. A native of Brooklyn, New York, Hall arrived in Ocean City after World War II and began buying undeveloped property that fronted the Sinepuxent Bay north of the bridge that led into town. Much of Hall's newly-acquired holdings were marshland, and he began to cut canals, upon which he then built bulkheads. Dredging fill dirt out of the marshes, he raised his newly-formed buildable plots seven feet above sea level. With the influx of vacationers sparked by the completion of the Chesapeake Bay Bridge, Hall had no problems selling his newly-created lots.

Hall was not alone in seeing the potential of Ocean City and other locations along the Delmarva coast, and the Maryland resort began to spread northward from the inlet toward the Delaware line. The older nineteenth- and early-twentieth-century wooden buildings with peaked roofs, tall windows and wide porches were joined with rectangular concrete structures that had more in common with a Florida boomtown. The new buildings boasted air conditioning, wall-to-wall carpeting and swimming pools—amenities that were unheard of in the area before World War II. Live bands that once entertained vacationers were replaced by television sets in the lobby, where vacationers eagerly sought a peek at their favorite programs.

North of Forty-First Street in Ocean City, the road leading through the dunes was punctuated by numerous new building projects. At the end of World War II, there were fewer than two hundred buildings between Ocean City and Fenwick Island, but after the Chesapeake Bay Bridge opened, motels, restaurants and other buildings were constructed on the sandy dunes. Not only was Ocean City bolstered by new construction, but the beach at the south end of town was also growing wider. The littoral drift of sand in that part of the Delmarva coast went from north to south, paralleling the beach. After the 1933 storm created the inlet, the new waterway was stabilized by stone groins that caused the sand to accumulate on the north side of the inlet, creating a broad, level beach. Unfortunately, the sand captured by the north groin of the inlet would have naturally replenished the beach at the north end of Assateague Island. Denied that sand, the Assateague beach began to erode westward.

At Fenwick Island, an abortive development at the start of the twentieth century resulted in the construction of the small Windrift hotel that catered to hunters in the winter and devotees of the surf in the summer. The road from Fenwick Island to the mainland via the Route 54 corridor remained problematic, and the area around the lighthouse remained an isolated and mostly undeveloped part of the Delmarva coast. There were a few vacation cottages near the Maryland line, including several wooden camp meeting buildings where people would gather for several days to listen to preachers, read the Bible and contemplate the state of their religion. Some of the attendees were housed in tents, and others built simple frame houses. At Fenwick Island, a wooden walkway ran perpendicular to the beach; when the camp meetings were held, crowds thronged the boardwalk, which ran from the camp circle to the beach. At most meetings, people promenaded around the camp circle, but at Fenwick Island, the grand procession of people was on the boardwalk and the beach.

When the coastal highway was built from Rehoboth to Ocean City, it was discovered that a number of the cottages at Fenwick Island were built on the right of way for the new road. The "squatters" were given an opportunity to purchase the nearby land for between $100 and $250. Some of the owners took advantage of the offer and moved their buildings, but there was no rush to purchase the lots. After the opening of the Chesapeake Bay Bridge, developers began to notice Fenwick Island, but the town leaders passed a number of zoning regulations that limited the height of buildings, restricted the types of businesses that could be established in the area and prohibited the construction of a boardwalk. The result was a quiet resort town with a cluster of small, mostly wooden buildings within sight of the lighthouse.

North of Fenwick Island, separated by about three miles of undeveloped oceanfront land owned by the state of Delaware, Richard Hall (the developer of many bayside lots in Ocean City) acquired a tract of land between the ocean and the coastal bay. To the north were the fringes of Bethany Beach. To the south, a World War II spotting tower stood amid the undeveloped dunes, and to the west was the edge of a marsh that was critical to Hall's projected development. In 1952, Hall climbed one of the dunes and proclaimed, "We'll call it South Bethany."

Ash Wednesday Nor'easter: 1962

Looking south from the Fenwick Island Lighthouse, a small cluster of buildings stand amid undeveloped dunes. *Courtesy of the Delaware Public Archives.*

As he did in Ocean City, Hall cut geometrically straight canals through the low-lying marshland, built bulkheads on the shoreline and used fill dirt to create high, firm ground on which he could offer buildable lots. After the completion of the Chesapeake Bay Bridge, a deluge of vacationers flooded to South Bethany, where they snapped up the lots at the rate of nearly one hundred per year. Development in the community of single-family homes was not confined to Hall's meticulously sculpted canals. Some vacationers wanted to be steps from the surf, and a decade after South Bethany was born, thirty-seven homes had been built directly on the dunes.

North of Hall's new development sat Bethany Beach, founded in the early twentieth century by a group led by Reverend F.D. Power, a minister at the Vermont Avenue Christian Church in Washington, D.C., who wanted to create a chautauqua-like place where believers could spend summers in Christian fellowship. The centerpiece of the new resort was a distinctive, octagon-shaped auditorium known as the Tabernacle. The building was designed with sides that could be opened to allow the sea breeze to cool the audience. The brown-shingled Tabernacle was used for Sunday services and chautauqua lectures. The building was also used for slide presentations, political meetings and musical concerts, and it hosted some of the first showings of motion pictures at the beach. Bethany Beach remained a quiet, uncrowded resort until the Chesapeake Bay Bridge opened, after which vacationers—many from Washington, D.C.—began to arrive in droves.

The opening of the bridge also fed the vacation community that had sprung up on the banks of the Indian River Inlet. Over the years, the persistent coastal currents and periodic storms had migrated the inlet to several locations on the coast. During colonial times, when rural roads in Delaware were unpaved and travel on land was slow and difficult, the Indian River Inlet was a vital link between the Atlantic Ocean and Delaware's coastal bays. Farmers who lived near the Rehoboth and Indian River bays used these waters to transport shingles cut from the Great Cypress Swamp, farm produce and other products.

During the War of 1812, the forty-gun frigate HMS *Nieman*, which was too large to navigate the inlet, anchored a safe distance from the beach and loaded several dozen sailors and marines into several boats. The flotilla of small craft used the inlet to enter the coastal bays, where the British soldiers burned several vessels and carried off a number of livestock. After the War of 1812, the inlet began to fill with silt; by the end of the nineteenth century, the waterway was little more than a wet spot in the sand. Without an outlet to the ocean, the coastal bays began to stagnate. The waters became choked with grasses and green algae that produced an overpowering stench. In the early twentieth century, several hundred farmers armed themselves with shovels and attacked the silt that blocked the inlet. For two days, the men assaulted the muck and created a shallow channel that allowed some water to flow from the bay to the ocean, but the wet sand on the new inlet's banks slid back into the watery ditch. When the shovel brigade returned for a second attempt, they dug a wider waterway, but it, too, quickly silted closed.

An attempt to use dynamite to blast a new inlet across the sand resulted in what historian Richard Carter called "the grandest explosion in the history of Sussex County" and opened a six-foot-deep and sixty-foot-wide channel between the coastal bays and the ocean. Within a short time, however, the sand on the banks of the new inlet began to slide back into the waterway, and the new inlet was closed. In 1934, federal funds were appropriated to create a permanent channel, and the new waterway was dug by dredges and earthmovers. As in Ocean City, the new inlet was reinforced by stone groins.

At the time that the inlet was reopened, construction began on a hard-surfaced highway along the coast. Given the history of shifting sands along

Ash Wednesday Nor'easter: 1962

the coast, questions were raised as to the advisability of building a permanent bridge over the water, but those concerns were put aside, and in 1934, a wooden bridge was constructed. This low, fixed bridge prevented most boats from using the waterway. The new highway was subject to washouts, and the low wooden bridge was soon replaced by a three-part structure with a center section that pivoted so vessels could sail to and from the Atlantic Ocean.

The new Indian River Inlet was located on a barren stretch of the Delaware coast, but the rejuvenated waterway opened new possibilities for coastal fishermen. After a delay caused by World War II, enterprising anglers exploited the inlet's potential. According to *The Public Press*, "In the spring of the year [1946] ex-GI John J. Marsh of Rehoboth Beach… formed the Indian River Yacht Club Basin Corporation, and rushed into action to dredge a harbor deep enough by July 1 to accommodate 50 deep-sea fishing craft…and hundreds of sportsmen today are still 'going out the inlet after a catch.'"

In cold winters, ice sometimes formed in the inlet and threatened to rip parts of the structure from its foundation. On February 10, 1948, large chunks of ice had filled the bad-tempered inlet, straining the supports of the bridge. Unaware of the precarious status of the bridge, a convoy of three trucks from the Electric Construction Company of Philadelphia attempted to cross the bridge. The first truck safely made it across, but the bridge collapsed, causing the second truck in the convoy to somersault into the inlet, killing three men. The third vehicle in the caravan could not stop in time, and it, too, plunged into the water, but this car landed upright, and the occupants managed to climb onto the roof, where they were rescued by the Coast Guard.

After the bridge collapse, a concrete and steel swing bridge was built over the inlet, and by the early 1950s, the Indian River Inlet had been opened for two decades. The tidal flow helped regenerate the oyster, crab and clam populations. A marina was built for fishing boats, and a small village of shanty houses and trailers were erected on the north shore of the inlet. Many of the buildings had no indoor plumbing and were served by customized outhouses, some with a little half-moon on the door. The current that ran through the inlet had led to the formation of a sandbar in the middle of the waterway; this constricted the channel and created strong rip currents. Kids with inner tubes thought it was great fun to ride these currents from one end of the inlet to the other. In 1952, the *New York Times* reported, "About seven miles below Dewey Beach is Indian River Inlet, one of the most popular fishing spots in the whole region. Here, more than 150 boats, from small outboards to big party boats, are available for fishing either in the ocean or Indian River Bay."

North of the inlet, Dewey Beach and Rehoboth did not experience the explosive growth that was ignited in Ocean City after the opening of the Chesapeake Bay Bridge. There was some new construction in both areas after the bay bridge opened, and as many as fifty thousand visitors total would crowd into the two towns on a summer weekend. Likewise, on the bayside of Cape Henlopen, Lewes Beach experienced limited growth during the late 1950s. Hemmed in by state-owned land south of Dewey Beach and Fort Miles north of Rehoboth, there was little oceanfront land in Delaware available for new construction. With the price of land rapidly escalating along the Maryland coast north of Ocean City, developers looked south of the inlet to Assateague Island.

ASSATEAGUE: ALL OF THE COMFORTS OF OCEAN CITY

In the late nineteenth century, when Ocean City was in its infancy, the Synepuxent Beach Company had proposed building a second resort on the island, but it failed to materialize. In the 1920s, developers proposed another resort named South Ocean City, but it, too, never advanced beyond the planning stage. By the end of World War II, Assateague was home to several small Coast Guard stations and a few primitive hunting lodges when developers began to cast their eyes on the last and largest undeveloped beach between North Carolina and Massachusetts. At the same time, conservationists were looking for ways to preserve the natural beauty of the island. In 1934, the year after the storm cut the inlet at Ocean City, the National Park Service surveyed lands along the Atlantic and Gulf coasts to identify possible national seashore recreation areas. Assateague Island, with its natural qualities, recreational possibilities and proximity to major cities was one of the twelve areas selected as potential seashore parks. For more than a decade, as the Great Depression wound down and World War II was fought, the wheels of government slowly turned, producing the inevitable reports on the feasibility of a national park on the Delmarva coast. After one such survey, Conrad L. Wirth, supervisor of recreation and land planning for the National Park Service, commented, "One excellent feature of the area is that all human use may be concentrated in the northern section [of the Delmarva coast] between Ocean City, Maryland, and Rehoboth Beach, Delaware....The 34-mile strip between Ocean City and Fishing Point [the south end of Assateague] could be preserved without any roads whatsoever."

In 1940, a bill was introduced into Congress to provide for the establishment of a Rehoboth-Assateague National Seashore. The bill called for federal acquisition of up to 75,000 acres of undeveloped land between Cape Henlopen and the south end of Assateague Island. Most of the land would be on the barrier islands, but one-fourth of the proposed purchase would be on the western shore of the coastal bays. The towns of Rehoboth, Bethany Beach, Ocean City and Chincoteague would be excluded from the projected national seashore.

While the National Park Service plan made its way through the federal bureaucracy, the U.S. Fish and Wildlife Service established Chincoteague National Wildlife Refuge on the south end of Assateague. In 1943, funds from the sale of migratory bird hunting and conservation stamps, popularly known as "duck stamps," were used to buy most of the Virginia portion of Assateague and a small tract near the border between Virginia and Maryland. Two hundred and seventy-five species of birds frequent the Chincoteague National Wildlife Refuge, and it has become one of the showplaces of the National Wildlife Refuge System.

Following World War II, the National Park Service lowered its goal for the establishment of a Rehoboth-Assateague National Seashore. The state of Delaware already owned much of the undeveloped oceanfront land between Cape Henlopen and Fenwick Island, and the Delaware State Park Commission was not enthusiastic about donating its holdings to the proposed national park. In addition, private investors, eyeing the impending completion of the Chesapeake Bay Bridge and the prospect of thousands of vacationers flooding the Atlantic coast, turned their attention to Assateague. Led by Leon Ackerman, a Marine veteran of both world wars, a group of investors bought fifteen miles of Assateague oceanfront land. The investors' newly acquired land was surveyed, subdivided and platted in preparation for development. A paved road, named Baltimore Boulevard, was constructed in the dunes parallel to the surf. Dubbing their Assateague project Ocean Beach, Ackerman's developers erected street signs for future roads that intersected with Baltimore Boulevard and placed enticing advertisements in major newspapers. According to an ad in the *Baltimore Sun* in 1952 (the year the Chesapeake Bay Bridge opened), "Ocean Beach, Maryland offers you a 'Lifetime of Vacations' on the great Atlantic Ocean." The ad went on to extol the natural assets of Assateague:

> *For summer fun, Ocean Beach has everything—cool ocean breezes, golden sunshine, exhilarating surf, sparkling blue ocean and wide, white sand beach offer you round-the-clock fun at this paradise of the Atlantic.... Ocean Beach is the only undeveloped ocean frontage on the Atlantic Coast where lots of nearly a half-acre can be obtained at prices within reach of the average man's pocketbook. Ocean Beach is a community beach, not a public beach. Every property owner will enjoy unlimited use of the entire 15 miles of beach.*

Building sites sized at 100 by 200 feet and costing only $650 could be had for only $100 down and $15 per month. With no bridge from Assateague to the mainland, the developers ferried potential buyers from the tip of Sinepuxent Neck across the narrow coastal bay to Assateague.

By the early 1960s, over three thousand people had bought nearly six thousand Ocean Beach lots. Most of the buyers were investors, and only thirty houses had been constructed. A National Park Service survey of Assateague completed in 1955 stated that the Maryland section of the island was "the site of one of the largest seashore developments along the Atlantic coast." The report concluded that the real estate development on Assateague appeared to preclude the development of a national seashore park.

In 1956, Ackerman donated 540 acres on the northern tip of Assateague overlooking the inlet to the state of Maryland in hopes that the state would build a bridge to the island. As developers worked to create a new resort on Assateague that would rival Ocean City, they were opposed by William E. Green, a blunt-talking advocate for maintaining the undeveloped nature of the island. In 1961, Ackerman's gift of land on the northern tip of the island paid off for him when the Maryland General Assembly authorized $1.5 million to construct a bridge that would give potential buyers easy access to the island. The developers appeared to have a clear path to develop the natural sands of Assateague when real storm clouds appeared on the horizon.

During the first week of March in 1962, the moon moved between the earth and the sun, creating a new moon. With the three celestial bodies in alignment, the gravitational tug of the sun and the moon on the oceans produced high tides everywhere on the planet. Veteran weather-watchers on Delmarva anticipated the usual high tides produced by a new moon, but they were surprised when a storm of unusual ferocity arrived along the coast. When two low-pressure disturbances combined to form a single nor'easter off the Atlantic coast, a high-pressure system over Canada prevented the

Ash Wednesday Nor'easter: 1962

storm from moving quickly northward; in some places, the storm-driven wind and waves would lash the coast through five high tides. The combined low-pressure disturbance was not a tropical storm, and therefore, the U.S. Weather Bureau did not dispatch any hurricane hunters to investigate it. Unlike hurricanes, which have compact, well-defined "eyes" with clearly delineated walls, the middle of a nor'easter is often rather ragged with an ill-defined center. The principal part of the March 1962 nor'easter was more egg-shaped than round and extended over much of the coast from Assateague to Cape Henlopen while it slowly made its way northward. Although there were some early weather satellites in orbit, the information they provided was meager, and the storm was tracked the old-fashioned way—by charting the winds and air pressure over areas where the storm had passed. This information was compiled too slowly to give any advance warning of the nor'easter's impact on the Delmarva coast.

The slow-moving storm was far enough off the coast to create a long fetch (the distance winds travel over open water) that enabled the hurricane-force winds to drive an enormous amount of water, unimpeded, to the coast. Combined with the extra high tide created by the new moon, the Atlantic Ocean rose up to deluge the Delmarva coast. The winds and water seemed to be at their height on March 7, Ash Wednesday, which gave the ferocious nor'easter its name.

At Chincoteague Island, the storm began with a light snow that quickly changed to rain, with the precipitation filling the coastal bay. Shielded by the southern end of Assateague, Chincoteague suffered comparably light wind damage, but the rising water ripped boats from their moorings and carried them into town, where the water was as much as six feet deep.

On Chincoteague, over 1,200 homes were damaged, and almost all of the cars were damaged by the flood. The storm decimated the island's thriving poultry industry, drowning 400,000 birds. With the causeway leading into town closed, helicopters evacuated people from Chincoteague to higher ground. Misty, a pony that became the subject of an award-winning children's book by Marguerite Henry, *Misty of Chincoteague*, waited out the storm in the kitchen of her owners after her barn was flooded.

On Assateague Island, volunteer firemen, who sold about 100 ponies per year to support their company, drove the herd of ponies to high ground on the south end of the island. The ponies were left to fend for themselves as the stormy surf rolled over the beach and, in some places, carried into Chincoteague Bay. The waters in the bay rose and inundated the marshes on its edges. The humans on Assateague evacuated the island, but the deer,

At Chincoteague in 1962, boats were left high and dry in the streets. *Courtesy of the Museum of Chincoteague Island.*

ponies and other wildlife gravitated to areas of high ground to wait out the storm as best they could. At Leon Ackerman's Ocean Beach development, the water breached the dunes and flooded into cottages that were meant to provide a "Lifetime of Vacations." Baltimore Boulevard was washed out, cut into sections and, in various parts, buried. Most of the dozen or so Assateague structures that escaped damage or destruction were older buildings on the bayside of the island.

At the northern tip of Assateague, the wind and water swept across the inlet separating the island from Ocean City. Unlike Assateague, where the storm was free to rearrange the sand and shoreline, in Ocean City development lined the beach for several dozen blocks, and the resort was home to about 1,500 permanent residents. When the rain began, many residents dismissed the storm as just another nor'easter, but when the wind and water continued to rise, many knew that they were in for something special. The ocean waves were ripping apart the boardwalk and sending debris into the streets, which were flooded with several feet of water. Buildings were carried

ASH WEDNESDAY NOR'EASTER: 1962

Flooding at Chincoteague was extensive in 1962. *Courtesy of the Museum of Chincoteague Island.*

At Chincoteague, some churchgoers arrived by boat. *Courtesy of the Museum of Chincoteague Island.*

off their foundations; sand was everywhere. The storm destroyed seventy-five homes and businesses in Ocean City and carried away from the beach a swath of sand two hundred and fifty feet wide and eight feet deep. With no way out of town, people took refuge in the upper floors of their homes and watched as debris floated by.

On Wednesday, March 7, the first National Guard troops arrived with amphibious vehicles to help with rescue operations. An informal network of CB radio operators helped coordinate rescue efforts, directing residents to hang white sheets from their windows as distress signals, and most residents were safely evacuated by Wednesday evening. Many of the evacuees were relocated to Buckingham Elementary School in Berlin. Lester Wise, a resident of Ocean City for nearly two decades, said that this was the worst storm he had ever seen, a sentiment echoed by many longtime residents. Wise commented, "I'm glad I'm in the life insurance business, not the property insurance business."

At the school, the refugees sat on civil defense cots, talked quietly and watched television on sets in the classrooms. Children played in the gym. The *Wilmington Morning News* reported, "In an area where traditions and mores crumble slowly, white and Negro refugees mingled without distinction." Many went to stay at private homes of friends or relatives. School officials, led by Principal Herman Sorin, prepared meals, and local residents arrived with Eastern Shore fried chicken. Refugees agreed: "It was worse than a hurricane."

In Ocean City, hundreds of buildings were damaged or destroyed. The storm ripped apart large sections of the boardwalk and sent the timbers floating through the town's flooded streets. At that time, the official town limits of Ocean City ended at Forty-First Street, but the building boom had spread development much farther northward. In some places, the storm breached the dunes and created temporary inlets—one of the largest of these was at Seventy-First Street.

A FEW CHUNKS OF CONCRETE SLAB

By the middle of the nineteenth century, the federal government and the U.S. Lighthouse Board had learned a thing or two about building lighthouses. In 1856, a beacon was authorized for Fenwick Island, and the army engineer who selected the site for the new tower must have had an experienced eye. He placed the tower about a half-mile from the surf, a short distance from a salt pond that bordered the beach and about midway between two ancient inlets that had silted closed. One of the old inlets was located a little north of Lewes Street in Fenwick Island, and a second inlet was located in Maryland less than a mile south of the Delaware border near 127th Street. The ground on which the lighthouse stood was firm and slightly higher than the surrounding terrain.

When the Fenwick Island Lighthouse was completed in 1859, the added elevation, however small, made the beacon visible to ships fifteen miles out at sea. The old inlets had disappeared by the early twentieth century, when the first vacationers appeared on Fenwick Island to build beach homes a short distance from the lighthouse. The resort's early wooden cottages lacked electricity, running water and other niceties, but these primitive accommodations were only a short walk from the surf.

When the coast was lashed by a strong storm in 1933, the owners of the cottages on Fenwick Island had little difficulty repairing their wooden beach houses. The number of cottages on the Fenwick Island beach had grown considerably when the Great Atlantic Hurricane of 1944 drove waves across the beach and inundated some of the cottages. Again, most owners quickly repaired their summer homes, and Fenwick Island continued to grow at a slow pace.

The roads leading to Fenwick Island had been considerably improved by 1952, when the Chesapeake Bay Bridge opened. Nona Brown reported in the *New York Times*: "Fenwick Island again is mostly a cottage community with a curious old lighthouse set a half mile back from the beach." During the 1950s, the deluge of vacationers spilled southward from Rehoboth, and Bethany Beach blossomed into a major resort. At the same time, Ocean City expanded northward as developers built on patches of beach during the town's steady march toward the Delaware line. The cottage community, with its historic lighthouse, could no longer resist development; by 1962, Fenwick Island was a pleasant community with most of the amenities of a small beachside resort.

When the Ash Wednesday storm arrived, the storm surge smashed through the dunes and flooded beach houses between the ocean and the coastal bay. As the storm began to abate, the late Mary Pat Kyle, a longtime coastal resident and the unofficial historian of Fenwick Island, made her way along Route 54 in an effort to reach her oceanfront property. Stopped by the high water near Keenwick West, Kyle crossed the road to a small cemetery that sat on a small elevation on the north side of the road. The beach was still some distance away, but Kyle could clearly see that most of Fenwick Island was submerged. According to Kyle, "Although we were approximately three miles inland, we could see huge breakers coming in to the shore and completely washing over the beach into the bay near the area of Fenwick Towers (built since the storm). The huge breaking waves are a sight I will never forget."

The old, dormant inlets that had once made Fenwick an island were reopened, and the ocean flowed freely into the coastal bays. During the height of the storm, forty waves surged across the dunes, flooding any buildings in their path. One area, however, remained secure. The Fenwick Island Lighthouse and the surrounding high ground on which the lighthouse keeper's nineteenth-century home stood were safely above the swirling waters—a testament to the army engineer's expert eye that led him to select the site for the lighthouse.

A few miles up the coast, South Bethany was ten years old when, in March 1962, the Ash Wednesday nor'easter began pumping water into the

The 1962 storm flooded Fenwick Island. *Courtesy of the Delaware Public Archives.*

coastal bays and into developer Richard Hall's carefully constructed canals. As happened in several places on the Delmarva coast, South Bethany went through five unusually high spring tides. The accumulated water flooded bayside streets, and the storm sent steady gale force winds and forty-foot waves across the beach, smashing buildings in their path. The damage throughout South Bethany was widespread, and along the oceanfront, it was total. All thirty-seven homes built on the dunes were destroyed. "The only clue my wife and I could find today to where our beach cottage had been," said South Bethany homeowner Garnett D. Horner, "was the two-inch well pipe, sticking up some three feet out of the sand."

North of Hall's development, Bethany Beach was more than fifty years older and had a substantial boardwalk and denser oceanfront development. Needless to say, the storm ripped up the planking for the boardwalk and left behind several neat rows of support pilings.

The destruction at South Bethany was almost total. *Courtesy of the Delaware Public Archives.*

Looking north toward Bethany Beach, this image shows the sand left behind from the 1962 storm. *Courtesy of the Delaware Public Archives.*

Looking south toward Bethany Beach as the cleanup began. *Courtesy of the Delaware Public Archives.*

ASH WEDNESDAY NOR'EASTER: 1962

Bethany Beach before the 1962 storm. The octagon-shaped Tabernacle is in the upper right corner. *Courtesy of the Delaware Public Archives.*

Bethany Beach after the 1962 storm. The site of the Tabernacle, in the upper right corner, has been wiped clean. *Courtesy of the Delaware Public Archives.*

At Bethany Beach, the Seaside Inn (*left center*) lost its ocean-facing front. *Courtesy of the Delaware Public Archives.*

All but one of twenty-nine oceanfront buildings were destroyed, and a number of structures farther from the beach were flooded and inundated with sand. On the northern edge of Bethany, the ocean water washed across the new four-lane road that had been built around the older section of the resort. In addition, the neat rows of barrack buildings at the National Guard camp were flooded. Fortunately, some of Bethany's older buildings had been moved back from the beach after earlier storms, and they survived.

FLOATING LIGHT POLES, BOATS AND DEBRIS

At the Indian River Inlet, the stone groins that stabilized the inlet interrupted the littoral flow of sand along the coast. Unlike Ocean City, where the sand migrated from north to south, in the area around the

Ash Wednesday Nor'easter: 1962

Indian River Inlet, the sand moved from south to north. Consequently, at the Indian River Inlet, the sand collected behind the south groin, causing the beach on the north side of the waterway to erode. Unfortunately, the small trailer community that developed after the inlet was reopened in the 1930s was on the north side of the inlet, and the narrow beach left it susceptible to storm damage.

As the Ash Wednesday storm pounded the coast, Coast Guardsmen Bill Mabry and a man known as "Curly" had become trapped on the north side of the inlet. Mabry and fellow Coast Guardsman Jim Overton were watching for boats in distress at the Indian River Inlet Yacht Basin when a member of the Delaware State Police arrived and asked if Mabry and Overton could help evacuate anyone in the trailers at the yacht basin to a building on high ground. Once this was done, Curly said that he needed to return to his trailer, and Mabry volunteered to go with him. They would not soon return. By late Tuesday, the ocean had breached the dunes, and it was flowing directly into the bay. The two men saw that it was impossible to get

The trailers near the Indian River Inlet after the 1962 storm. *Courtesy of the Delaware Public Archives.*

back to high ground, and they sought refuge in one of the few trailers that had not been carried off its foundation by the rising waters and high winds. According to the *Delaware Coast Press*, "All around their trailer, light poles, boats, debris, and wood were floating by. Afraid that the trailer might start to blow around, they opened all the doors and windows to let the water run through the trailer rather than take the chance of it catching their trailer, like others, and float it about."

Inside the trailer, the water continued to rise. One of the men retreated to a table and the other climbed a stepladder to keep their heads above the cold water. Early Wednesday, Bill heard a helicopter, and he felt his way to the top of a door. Plunging into the water, he swam through the door and climbed onto the roof. Desperately, he waved to the helicopter, but those aboard the chopper failed to notice him.

Around two o'clock p.m. on Wednesday, a rescue crew from the high ground was able to reach Mabry and Curly and get them to safety. They had been in the water for almost nineteen hours. The two men were airlifted by the National Guard helicopter to Beebe Hospital. Having survived the worst storm to hit the Delaware coast, Mabry commented, "I've heard of people being cold but I was numb. I would never want to go through anything like it again. My only regrets are for the people who lost property, and for the very few who lost their lives."

REHOBOTH: BELIES THE IMAGINATION

North of the Indian River Inlet, where the state owned several miles of undeveloped land, the storm eroded the dunes and drove the surf across the coastal highway, reaching the coastal bay in some places. The high water carried an enormous amount of sand with it and deposited it on the coastal road. The old Indian River Inlet Life-Saving Station, consisting of a main boathouse that contained sleeping quarters for the surfmen and several smaller structures, had been taken over by the Coast Guard in the early twentieth century, and the nineteenth-century wooden structure survived the storm. The waves that lapped about the station left several feet of sand in and around the buildings.

The state-owned land ended at Dewey Beach, which always prided itself as being the less-restrictive and less-developed neighbor to Rehoboth. Nonetheless, the storm found numerous structures at Dewey Beach

Ash Wednesday Nor'easter: 1962

The Coast Guard Station at Indian River Inlet (formerly the Indian River Life-Saving Station) surrounded by sand. *Courtesy of the Delaware Public Archives.*

to flood, rip apart and destroy. As in other places along the coast, the oceanfront buildings suffered the most, but Dewey Beach sat on a narrow neck of land pinched between the northern end of Rehoboth Bay and the ocean. In several places, the rising water flowed directly between the ocean and the bay. Bellevue Street resembled a Venetian canal, with water flowing past the landmark Bottle and Cork Taproom, which had catered to servicemen from Fort Miles during World War II and would one day earn a reputation as the "Greatest Rock and Roll Bar in the World." On the bayside at Dewey Beach, the boat docks were ripped apart, and small boats piled up one on top of another.

At Rehoboth Beach, the decade of growth that followed the opening of the Chesapeake Bay Bridge had filled in many of the oceanfront lots and created a nearly continuous stretch of development that lined the boardwalk. As with the other resorts along the coast, the decking of the boardwalk was shattered, and many of the timbers were carried

Dewey Beach streets were flooded from the ocean to the bay. *Courtesy of the Delaware Public Archives.*

The boardwalk at Rehoboth Beach in the early hours of the 1962 storm. *Courtesy of the Delaware Public Archives.*

into Rehoboth's streets. A recently installed wide concrete section of the boardwalk at the end of Rehoboth Avenue was torn apart by the endless pounding of the storm-driven waves.

The stone WCTU fountain, a favorite watering place for vacationers at the end of Rehoboth Avenue, and the boardwalk lay in pieces. On the south end of the boardwalk, a small section was still standing, but it was so battered that it was impossible to repair. Most of the buildings in the oceanfront block paralleling the boardwalk were beaten to splinters or completely disappeared, swallowed up by the roaring ocean waves. The Pink Pony, a popular boardwalk nightclub, was gone, with only a few pilings sticking out of the sand to indicate where it once was. When the surf undermined the foundation of the Sussex Apartments, the building gave way, and the line of boardwalk shops that fronted the apartments were bashed and beaten to pieces.

The three hotels adjacent to the boardwalk, with their excellent views of the ocean and ready access to the surf, were prime lodging places in

The 1962 storm left a field of broken timbers at Rehoboth Beach. *Courtesy of the Delaware Public Archives.*

The Atlantic Sands Motel lost a significant part of its interior rooms. *Courtesy of the Rehoboth Historical Society.*

Rehoboth, but the storm did not treat them kindly. The wing of the Atlantic Sands, a modern concrete building that fronted the boardwalk, collapsed under the fury of the storm.

At the corner of Rehoboth Avenue and the boardwalk, the surfside of the popular Belhaven, with its open veranda, where politicians gathered on July 4 to discuss the topics of the day with their constituents, was destroyed. The Henlopen Hotel was a fixture at Rehoboth since the early days of the town. First built as a wooden structure with double-decker wraparound porches that faced the beach, the Henlopen was rebuilt and extensively renovated several times. In 1962, the hotel had shed the Victorian look of the original hotel and the pre–World War II Spanish look in favor of an up-to-date rectangular look. In March 1962, the Henlopen Hotel was the grande dame of Rehoboth when the waves began to tear out its modern facade. Situated at the northern end of the boardwalk, where the waves undermined the foundation of the Stuart Kingston Galleries, the Henlopen Hotel had its oceanfront façade ripped away as the storm knocked in its front and left the

Ash Wednesday Nor'easter: 1962

The Henlopen Hotel with its oceanfront gone. *Courtesy of the Delaware Public Archives.*

building leaning back as if shying away from another blow. Rooms that had once provided an excellent view of the Atlantic were now part of the debris tossed about by the surf.

Two of the most popular attractions on the boardwalk, Funland and Dolle's Candyland, were battered almost beyond recognition. Water cascaded into the streets facing the ocean, carrying with it boardwalk timbers, building fragments and—above all—tons of sand. Both Silver Lake and Lake Gerar, on either end of the resort, were filled to overflowing, and unlike during the 1933 hurricane, the ocean cut a path through the dunes to roll unimpeded into Silver Lake.

Most houses in Rehoboth lost phone and electric service early in the storm, but some maintenance crews began to work even as the rain continued to fall. On Thursday morning, a fleet of about a dozen telephone repair trucks rode into Rehoboth to reestablish communication with the outside world.

On the bayside of Cape Henlopen, Lewes Beach was flooded with up to six feet of water from the bayfront to the canal. Savannah Road was inundated

Above: Flooding on Savannah Road cut off access to Lewes Beach. *Courtesy of the Delaware Public Archives.*

Opposite, top: Downtown Milton after the 1962 storm. *Courtesy of the Delaware Public Archives.*

Opposite, bottom: The Grier house in Rehoboth. *Courtesy of the Delaware Public Archives.*

a short distance after it crossed the canal and made travel impossible except by amphibious vehicles used by the National Guard. At least fifty people from Lewes Beach were evacuated to the Lewes Fire Hall.

The town of Lewes, however, sits on a low bluff that borders the canal, and it escaped major damage. Streets were flooded in some Delaware inland towns, such as Milton; farther north, the Ash Wednesday storm inflicted significant damage along the New Jersey coast and in New England before moving out to sea.

The March nor'easter was credited with causing forty deaths, but none were more heartbreaking than the calamity that befell the Waters family of Bowers Beach, about twenty-five miles north of Lewes. The Waters's home was near the shore of the Delaware Bay and only twenty feet from the swollen St. Jones River. John A. Waters awoke at 5:30 on Tuesday morning

Ash Wednesday Nor'easter: 1962

to discover that high water was sweeping across the lowlands that surrounded his home. Immediately sensing the danger, he roused his pregnant wife, their seven children and Mamie Whittington, his blind mother-in-law. The family quickly dressed and got into their car, but when Waters saw that he could not drive through the high water, he decided to wait for the tide to recede. Spotting a possible refuge, he took his wife and his oldest son, thirteen-year-old John Jr., to a nearby oyster house that sat on pilings. As Waters started back for the other children and his mother-in-law, the water lifted the car free of the ground, and it began to drift away. One of the children, seven-year-old Eugene, tried to crawl through one of the vehicle's windows, but he was carried away with the car. Shortly afterward, the Dover Fire Company and the Delaware National Guard arrived in a rescue boat and took Waters, his wife and John Jr. to safety. The men of the National Guard were able to reach the Waters's car, and they pulled Whittington and Alisa, age nine, from the submerged car and rushed them to the Kent General Hospital, where they recovered. The five other children drowned.

On Thursday, March 8, 1962, the *Delaware Coast Press* reported: "Disaster, without any forewarning, struck the Rehoboth Beach, Lewes and Dewey Beach area on Tuesday and Wednesday of this week, causing damage to properties estimated at over $10 million. The havoc was so great it belies the imagination."

CHAPTER 7
The New Reality

REBUILDING

By Friday, March 9, 1962, the storm had finally moved away from the Delmarva coast. After the rain stopped, the winds diminished and the waves flattened, residents of the coastal communities emerged to inspect the surreal beachfront. Familiar buildings were now a pile of debris, others were knocked off their foundations and some were simply gone. Rows of neatly spaced pilings hinted at where boardwalks once stood in Ocean City, Bethany and Rehoboth.

The water receded, but it left a nasty layer of mud with an overlay of sand, as if the coast had been visited by a perverse blizzard that deposited several feet of sand on the coast instead of dropping snow. To avoid being swamped by sightseers, the authorities along Delmarva limited access to the coastal communities to those who could show proof that they were residents of the affected towns.

In general, the storm had pushed the beach one hundred feet westward, and work crews in the developed communities began to push the sand back out of the streets toward the surf. In Maryland, workers cleared the sand from major streets as they worked their way northward toward Delaware, where crews were doing similar work. Between Fenwick Island and Rehoboth, the coastal highway had been overwashed by the ocean or the bay or, in some spots, by both.

At Bethany, rows of pilings indicate where the boardwalk once stood. *Courtesy of the Delaware Public Archives.*

Coastal Highway (*running across the center of this photo*) with a thick covering of sand. *Courtesy of the Delaware Public Archives.*

The New Reality

The destruction near the ocean was nearly complete, but buildings a block away from the surf were relatively undamaged. *Courtesy of the Delaware Public Archives.*

In several places, the storm had carried away or undermined the roadbed. A week after the storm, the fate of Route 14 (as the coastal highway was known at that time) was much in question. At a meeting of the Delaware State Highway Commission in Dover on March 14, it was suggested that the coastal road be abandoned in favor of a route on the western shore of the Indian River and Rehoboth bays. The *Delaware Coast Press* reported, "Originally, the State Highway Department planned to make Route 14 a dual highway....Now the question is not one of dualization so much as the advisability of reconstructing Route 14 to the same condition as it was before the storm."

The newspaper went on to editorialize:

> *There should be no question in anyone's mind of the necessity of rebuilding the ocean highway, but which of two alternatives is the most feasible.... We think it worthwhile to save our beaches between the ocean and the bay*

and to continue plans for a dual highway on it, if for no other reason than there had been an assessed property tax valuation to the county and state of about $50,000,000. Over a period of years this value kept increasing and in turn increased the "tax-take" of the county and state. Our ocean strip more than paid its way until the storm....The end result of restoring our beach land, it seems to us, would more than justify the cost. Consider the property tax dollars and the tourist trade dollars our beachlands bring into the coffers of Delaware.

As homeowners tended to their damaged beach houses, government authorities quickly decided to rebuild the coastal highway and the resort boardwalks in Maryland and Delaware. Frank H. Buck, Rehoboth Beach city manager, echoed the attitude prevalent in all the Delmarva resorts: "We will drive to get everything possible ready by the summer season."

Once the storm damage was repaired, the resorts would be open for business as if nothing had happened. Vohnnie Pearson, a civil engineer and

Crews cleaning the tons of sand from Coastal Highway. *Courtesy of the Delaware Public Archives.*

The New Reality

Clearing the debris from Rehoboth. *Courtesy of the Delaware Public Archives.*

oceanographer with the Delaware State Highway Department, declared, "That kind [of storm] comes one in half a century—on the average." Delaware state geologist Dr. Johan J. Groot saw stumps, once part of a forest along the beaches, that were uncovered when the sand was washed away from the storm. Groot said that the storm might not be an isolated event: "It might all be inter-related with the gradual changes that are occurring to the coast line."

While the resort communities worked to get things back to normal by the opening of the 1962 summer season, south of the Ocean City inlet, on Assateague, the storm had returned the island to its normal, natural state. By wiping the island clean of the Ocean Beach development and other nascent efforts to develop the island, the storm ended all hopes to turn Assateague into another Ocean City. The Ash Wednesday storm energized Secretary of the Interior Stewart L. Udall to revive the long-proposed Assateague National Seashore. With the support of Maryland governor J. Millard Tawes, another study was commissioned, and in April 1963, it recommended the

Tons of sand are pushed back toward the surf in Dewey Beach. *Courtesy of the Delaware Public Archives.*

establishment of Assateague Island National Seashore, which would be administered by the National Park Service. There followed several years of wrangling, but in the end, Assateague was spared further development, and Assateague Island National Seashore became a reality.

STORMS AFTER 1962

After the Ash Wednesday nor'easter, it did not take long for another strong storm to strike the coast. In November 1962, winds gusting to seventy-five miles per hour lashed the Delmarva coast; fortunately, high tides and peak winds did not coincide, and the coast escaped without major damage. Three weeks later, high tides during a second storm swept much of the rebuilt beach in Rehoboth and Bethany out to sea. In Fenwick Island, the storm had the opposite effect, depositing a layer of sand up to three feet thick on the streets. Two years later, in January 1964, a storm-generated high tide flooded streets in the Delmarva resorts, but damage was not as great as it could have been, since many houses in the flooded area had not been rebuilt after the Ash Wednesday storm.

During the remainder of the 1960s and throughout the 1970s, the coast was hit by a succession of nor'easters and tropical storms that flooded streets and tore down tree limbs, but the damage done by these storms was minor compared to the results of the 1962 nor'easter. Coastal residents, however, were reminded what damage high wind and water could do; whenever a strong storm was forecasted, they filled bathtubs with water, took furniture off porches and boarded up windows and doors. Luggage and bags were filled with essential items so that they could be quickly grabbed in the event of a hasty evacuation.

In September 1985, Hurricane Gloria, a Category 4 storm and one of the strongest to hit the U.S. coastline so far north, came ashore at Cape Hatteras, North Carolina. As the storm approached the Delmarva coast, evacuations were ordered, and most vacationers abandoned the resorts for higher ground inland. Some store clerks and others, however, did not make it out soon enough, and they were advised to shelter in place. Several days later, Stewart Dobson wrote in the *Ocean City Times*, "Hurricane Gloria, potentially one of the most vicious storms of the century, a cyclonic monster fueled by 130 mph winds, fired its shot at Ocean City Friday [September 27] morning…and missed." Gloria sideswiped the barrier islands and did some damage to boardwalks and buildings, but flooding was minor, and the cost of the damage was far below the possible $1 billion that the National Weather Service had predicted.

MOVING THE OCEAN

The storms that followed the Ash Wednesday nor'easter were a constant reminder that nature was constantly reshaping the Delmarva barrier islands. Nonetheless, this did not slow the pace of development, and within a decade of the 1962 storm, many high-rise condominiums were built on the beach between 94th and 118th Streets. The broad stretches of natural dunes that once characterized the Maryland coast were filled in with new construction, resulting in a resort town that stretched from the Ocean City inlet to the Delaware line. The development of Ocean City was repeated on a smaller scale in the Delaware coastal towns. On Assateague Island, the establishment of a Maryland state park just south of the Ocean City inlet and a national seashore on the rest of the island blocked development of one of the few remaining natural beaches in the mid-Atlantic area. As the number of vacationers continued to increase at Maryland and Delaware coastal resorts, the popularity of the parks on Assateague also increased, which led to the development of parking lots, campgrounds and other support facilities.

After the 1914 storm in Rehoboth destroyed the boardwalk and damaged beachfront homes on Surf Avenue, many homeowners opted to move their buildings back from the dunes to what they considered safer locations. This was repeated in Bethany and elsewhere. Moving inland had been a viable option when the beach homes were small wooden structures and land was readily available, but as the resorts grew, land became scarce and buildings became taller, heavier and more difficult to move. In Ocean City, some of the condominiums were twenty stories high and faced a diminishing beach; if the building could not be moved, the only viable option was to move the ocean eastward. By the late 1960s, a replenishment project to widen the beach in the Maryland resort was mired in government red tape. In 1970, Harry Kelley, the flamboyant mayor of Ocean City, became frustrated with the delays. He decided to act and led a squad of bulldozers that rode into the surf. Turning to face the depleted barrier island, the earthmovers pushed sand back onto the beach. Although environmentalists complained that the bulldozers were doing more harm than good, Kelley kept his bulldozers rolling until a beach replenishment program was devised that pumped offshore sand onto the Ocean City beach.

Coastal replenishment programs aim to rebuild the beaches and dunes that serve as natural protection for the buildings near the ocean. Dredging vessels suck up sand from the ocean floor at locations one to two miles offshore and then pump it onto the beach through huge pipes. As the sand is pumped, bulldozers smooth it into a wide, gradually rising beach. After sand is pumped onto the beach and graded, the artificial dune is planted with grasses to stabilize the sand. Designated walkways encourage beachgoers to avoid trampling on the dunes and damaging the grasses. As beach replenishment projects became more common, they became more accepted and are now a permanent part of the beach landscape in the resort towns in Maryland and Delaware.

The replenished beaches are not without their critics. When a storm washes away a replenished dune, some skeptics complain that valuable tax money was washed away with the sand. On the other hand, proponents

The New Reality

Ocean City condominiums now sit behind rebuilt dunes and a wide replenished beach. *Photo by Michael Morgan.*

point out that the replenished dunes were always intended to be temporary. The energy that a storm expends eroding a replenished beach is energy that would have been used to batter down a boardwalk, a beach cottage or a condominium. The tens of millions of dollars that it costs to periodically rebuild the beach pales in comparison to the hundreds of millions of dollars of damage that would be done to the oceanfront resorts if the beaches were not replenished. Owners of ground-floor units in some condominiums complained that their view of the ocean was blocked by the artificial dunes, even though their units were the most at risk.

Surfers, experts in observing waves and their behavior, point out that the steep slopes of many replenishment projects cause the waves to break so close to shore that the rebuilt beaches are unsuitable for surfing. Surfers now congregate at Cape Henlopen State Park, the south side of the Indian River Inlet and Assateague, where beaches have not been replenished.

State and national park officials have attempted to keep their beaches natural, and they avoided beach replenishment—with a few major exceptions. In Delaware, after the Indian River Inlet was made permanent

The wide beach on Assateague National Seashore. *Photo by Michael Morgan.*

by the construction of stone groins on either side of the waterway, a low, wooden bridge was built over the inlet. The highway leading to the bridge was subject to washouts, and the bridge was replaced by a three-part structure with a center section that pivoted so that vessels could sail through the inlet. In 1948, this structure had collapsed, and a concrete and steel swing bridge was built over the inlet. After the Ash Wednesday storm, this structure was replaced with a higher span, which was widened in 1976. By the 1990s, the currents coursing through the inlet had scoured so much sand from the foundation of the bridge that the structure needed to be replaced. The bridge project suffered from design changes, contract difficulties and the settlement of the underground soils. The new bridge was finally opened in 2012, but the littoral drift of sand caused the sand to build up on the jetties on the south side of the inlet, resulting in an erosion of sand on the north side of the inlet and threatening the approach road to the bridge. To protect this road, the beach was replenished, and measures were put into place to pump sand around the jetty to replicate the natural flow and help maintain the sand on the north side of the Indian River Inlet.

The New Reality

At the Ocean City inlet, the littoral flow of sand is in the opposite direction, which causes the sand to build up on the north side of the inlet, creating a broad beach. On the south side, the northern tip of Assateague Island is deprived of sand, and the coast has migrated westward the length of nearly four football fields. Geologists predicted that the northern part of the island was in danger of fragmenting when future storms created new inlets. The disintegration of the northern tip of Assateague would have enormous impact on the coastal bays and the Ocean City inlet. In the 1990s, a plan to salvage the northern end of Assateague was developed. In 2002, the beach was rebuilt using offshore sand that was pumped onto the beach and smoothed by bulldozers to create a wide beach and a higher line of dunes. Two years later, a program was initiated to replicate the natural flow of sand that had been interrupted by the construction of the inlet groins. Twice a year, sand is pumped from offshore areas near Ocean City to the surf zone south of the inlet. The littoral currents distribute this sand on the Assateague beach.

Wild ponies continue to graze on Assateague Island. *Photo by Michael Morgan.*

In Virginia, at Wallops Island, a rocket-testing facility was established in 1945 and eventually became the site of the National Aeronautics and Space Administration (NASA) Goddard Space Flight Center's Wallops Flight Facility. Rocket launch pads and support structures were engineered to survive explosions from rocket malfunctions and could generally withstand high winds from hurricanes or nor'easters. Some of the launch pads, however, are located within several hundred yards of the surf, and to protect these facilities from beach erosion, a steel sheet pile seawall was built in 1956. Three years later, wood groins were constructed to catch the littoral drift of sand. When the Ash Wednesday storm breached the seawall, it was abandoned in favor of a plied rock wall; in 2012, offshore sand was pumped in front of the area of the rocks to replenish the beach.

THREE LITTLE PIGS

It has been nearly half a millennium since Verrazano sailed along the shores of the Delmarva coast. During the three centuries that followed his epic voyage, European colonists, accompanied by their African slaves, settled on the Delmarva mainland, leaving wind and waves to sculpt the barrier islands as had been done for eons. In the early nineteenth century, storm-driven shipwrecks led to the construction of the Delaware Breakwater, interrupting the flow of sand around Cape Henlopen and accelerating the westward migration of the coast at the northern tip of Delmarva. After the ice storm of 1888, a second breakwater was built, further exacerbating the erosion on Cape Henlopen. When a storm created an inlet on the south edge of Ocean City, the waterway was stabilized, thwarting the forces of nature that periodically opened and closed inlets the length of Delmarva. After the Ash Wednesday nor'easter devastated the oceanfront communities, they were rebuilt bigger and stronger than ever. The 1962 storm eventually led to the creation of beach replenishment projects that pushed the ocean back from the new multimillion-dollar buildings that sat on the sand.

The efforts to combat the erosive effects of the wind and waves parallels the old English fairy tale of the three little pigs. One pig built a house of straw, another of sticks and the third of bricks. The big bad wolf huffed and puffed and blew down the first two houses but was unable to blow down the third house. The wolf, however, was able to get in through the brick house's chimney, and only a fortuitous flame in the fireplace was able to drive him

The New Reality

away. The progression from the bark and sapling structures of the Native Americans through the wooden houses of the early colonists to the reinforced concrete buildings of today echoes the three little pigs' efforts to thwart the wind of the big bad wolf. However, like the wolf, nature finds other ways to attack those who dare to build along the coast. As the nor'easter in 1962 demonstrated, water that undermines foundations and inundates buildings can be as destructive as wind.

To combat storms, stronger building codes and beach replenishment projects help mitigate the effects of wind and water. Evacuation routes have also been established and clearly marked, but as veteran visitors to the coast know, traffic on these routes on summer weekends is often gridlocked even in clear weather. As the year-round population of coastal Delmarva grows, there are more people who have not experienced the fury of a hurricane or the power of a nor'easter. Fortunately, improved weather forecasting capabilities and smartphones enable those in threatened areas to receive up-to-the-minute storm information. When the next Vagabond Hurricane or Ash Wednesday storm hits the coast, it should not be a surprise, and good forecasting should allow visitors and residents time to evacuate before a storm arrives.

Rehoboth, 1962. *Courtesy of the Rehoboth Historical Society.*

After the 1962 Ash Wednesday storm, geologist Johan Groot commented that the Delaware coast was sinking as much as a foot per century. He also said that sea level has been rising and warned that, "We must all think of the future." In the years to come, the combined effect of the sinking land and the rising sea will result in storms that may be bigger and more devastating than any that have hit the Delmarva coast in the past. Visitors and residents would do well to heed the Hawaiian saying: "Never turn your back on the ocean."

Bibliography

Abplanalp, Jean Murdock, and Barbara Quillen Dougherty. *Dewey Beach History & Tales*. Milton, DE: Harold E. Dukes Jr., publisher, nd.
Annual Report of the United States Life-Saving Service for the Fiscal Year ending June 30, 1888, Washington, DC: Government Printing Office, 1889.
Archdeacon, Herbert. "The Breakwaters." *Journal of the Lewes Historical Society*, Vol. 3, November 2000.
Assateague Island National Seashore North End Restoration Project. https://www.nps.gov/asis/learn/nature/upload/ProjectIntroduction.pdf.
Beach, John (Jack) W. *The Cape Henlopen Lighthouse*. Dover, DE: Henlopen Publishing Co., 1970.
———. *This Was Rehoboth Beach, Flotsam, Jetsam and Trivia*. Lewes, DE: Media Associates, 1993.
Bethany Beach Landowners Association. *A Walk Through History, 1901–1976*. http://www.bethany-beach.net/history.htm.
Bittof, N.H. "I Remember…A Much Different Ocean City." *The Sunday Sun Magazine*, June 5, 1966.
Brinkley, M. Kent. *The Hurricane History of Colonial Virginia to 1775*. https://facultystaff.richmond.edu/~wgreen/ejem0102.htm.
Brittingham, Hazel D. *Lantern on Lewes, Where the Past Is Present*. Lewes, DE: Lewestown Publishers, 1998.
Bryant, Tracey L., and Jonathan R. Pennock. *The Delaware Estuary: Rediscovering a Forgotten Resource*. Newark: University of Delaware Sea Grant College Program, 1998.

BIBLIOGRAPHY

Building for Tomorrow, The Indian River Inlet Bridge Newsletter. Delaware Department of Transportation, May 2011.

Carter, Dick. *The History of Sussex County*. Rehoboth Beach, DE: Community News Corporation, 1976.

Charles, Joan. *Mid-Atlantic Shipwreck Accounts to 1899*. Hampton, VA: Privately printed, 1997.

Coggeshall, George. *Thirty-Six Voyages in Various Parts of the World*. New York: self-published, 1858.

Corddry, Mary. *City on the Sand, Ocean City Maryland and the People Who Built It*. Centreville, MD: Tidewater Publishers, 1991.

Cox, S.S. "The Life Saving Service." *The North American Review*, May 1881.

Crowell, John S. *Affidavit, March 15, 1888*. Lewes Historical Society Archives.

Delaware: A Guide to the First State. Federal Writers' Project. Dover: Delaware Heritage Press, 2006.

Delaware Coast Storm Damage Report. Newark, DE: Department of Geography, 1977.

Delaware's Changing Shore Line. Dover: Delaware State Planning Office, 1976.

Dennis, W.A., G.A. Lanan, and R.A. Dalrymple. "Chapter 75 Case Studies of Delaware's Tidal Inlets: Roosevelt and Indian River Inlets." http://journals.tdl.org/icce/index.php/icce/article/viewFile/3337/3005.

Dennison, William C., et al. *Shifting Sands*. N.p.: IAN Press, 2009.

de Vries, David Pietersz. *Voyages from Holland to America*. http://134.76.163.65/agora_docs/4309TABLE_OF_CONTENTS.html.

Doughty, Frances Albert. "Life at a Life-Saving Station." *Catholic World*, July 1897.

Gentile, Gary. *Shipwrecks of Delaware and Maryland*. Philadelphia: Gary Gentile Productions, 1990.

George, Pam. *Shipwrecks of the Delaware Coast Tales of Pirates, Squalls & Treasure*. Charleston, SC: The History Press, 2010.

Hamline, Rev. L.L., ed. *The Ladies' Repository*, Vol. 3. Cincinnati: R.P. Thompson, 1843.

Hardaway, C. Scott, Jr. *Wallops Assateague Chincoteague Inlet (WACI) Geologic and Coastal Management Summary Report*. Virginia Institute of Marine Science and Accomack-Northampton Planning District Commission, n.p.: 2015.

Hugg, David S., III, et al. *Coastal Storm Damage, 1923–1974*. Newark: University of Delaware, 1977.

Hurley, George, and Suzanne Hurley. *Ocean City, A Pictorial History*, Virginia Beach: Donning Company, 1979.

BIBLIOGRAPHY

———. *Shipwrecks and Rescues Along the Barrier Islands of Delaware, Maryland and Virginia*. Virginia Beach: The Donning Company, 1984.
Jordan, Francis. *Aboriginal Fishing Stations on the Coast of the Middle Atlantic States*. Philadelphia: New Era Printing Company, 1906.
———. *The Remains of an Aboriginal Encampment at Rehoboth Delaware*. Philadelphia: Numismatic and Antiquarian Society of Philadelphia, 1880.
Keesey, Lori. "Recollections of Ocean City." *Maryland Magazine*, Summer 1986.
Kimball, Summer L. *Organization and Methods of the United States Life-Saving Service*. Washington, D.C.: Government Printing Office, 1894.
King, David B., Jr., et al. *Storm Damage Reduction Project Design for Wallops Island, Virginia*. Norfolk, VA: Corps of Engineers, 2011.
Kyle, Mary Pat. *Fenwick Island, Delaware: A Brief History*. Charleston, SC: The History Press, 2008.
Little Owl (Charles C. Clark IV). *The Nanticoke, Heartland of Del-Mar-Va*. Sunshine, 1987.
Mackintosh, Barry. *Assateague Island National Seashore, An Administrative History*. Washington, D.C.: National Park Service, 1982.
Manufacturer and Builder, February 1871.
———, May 1876.
Marye, William B. "The Sea Coast of Maryland." *Maryland Historical Magazine*, June 1945.
Matthews, Katie Gaskings, and William Russell. *Worcester County, A Pictorial History*. Norfolk, VA: The Donning Company, 1985.
McBee, Avery. "Ocean City Standing By for Summer Population." *Sunday Sun Magazine*, May 15, 1938.
Meehan, James D. *Bethany Beach Memoirs...A Long Look Back*. Bethany Beach, DE: Harold E. Dukes Jr., 1998.
———. *Rehoboth Beach Memoirs...From Saints to Sinners*. Bethany Beach, DE: Harold E. Dukes Jr., 2000.
———. *When Life was a Day at the Beach*. Bethany Beach, DE: Harold E. Dukes Jr., 2007.
Merryman, James H. "The United States Life-Saving Service." *Scribner's Monthly*, January 1880.
Morison, Samuel Eliot. *The European Discovery of America, The Northern Voyages*. New York: 1971.
Murphy, Henry C. *The Voyages of Verrazzano*. New York: 1875.
NOAA History. *The 1943 "Surprise" Hurricane*. http://www.history.noaa.gov/stories_tales/surprise.html.

Bibliography

———. *History of Hurricane Names.* http://www.nhc.noaa.gov/aboutnames_history.shtml.

Noble, Dennis L. *That Others Might Live: The U.S. Life-Saving Service, 1878–1915.* Annapolis, MD: Naval Institute Press, 1994.

A Paradise for Gunners and Anglers. Philadelphia: Philadelphia, Wilmington & Baltimore Railroad Company, 1883.

Pearson, Eric A. *Bits & Pieces on Fabulous Cape Henlopen.* Lewes, DE: Eric Pearson, 1991.

Pepper, Dorothy. "The Fenwick Island Lighthouse." *Del-Mar-Va Heartland,* Fall 1991.

Pyle, Howard. "Among the Sand Hills." *Harper's New Monthly Magazine,* September 1892.

———. "Chincoteague, The Island of Ponies." *Scribner's Monthly,* April 1877.

———. "A Peninsular Canaan." *Harper's New Monthly Magazine,* July 1879.

Register of Pennsylvania, Vol. 1, Philadelphia: 1828.

Scharf, J. Thomas. *History of Delaware.* Philadelphia: J.L. Richards and Co., 1888.

Scuttlebutt. Newsletter of the Ocean City Museum Society, Inc., Spring 2014.

Seventeenth Century Virginia Hurricanes. http://www.wpc.ncep.noaa.gov/research/roth/va17hur.htm.

Shanks, Ralph, Wick York, and Lisa Woo Shanks, ed. *U.S. Life-Saving Service: Heroes, Rescues and Architecture of the Early Coast Guard.* Petaluma, CA: Costano Books, 1998.

Smith, John. *The Generall Historie of Virginia, New England and The Summer Isles.* Glasgow: John MacLehose and Sons, 1907.

South Bethany Historical Society. *The Best Little Beach in Delaware.* Marceline, MO: Walsworth Print Group, 2014.

Spears, John R. "Sand-Waves at Henlopen and Hatteras." *Scribner's Magazine,* July–December 1890.

Stevenson, Jay. *Rehoboth of Yesteryear,* Vol. 2. Millsboro, DE: 1981.

Taylor, Bayard. "Down the Eastern Shore." *Harper's New Monthly Magazine,* September 1871.

Touart, Paul Baker. *Along the Seaboard Side: The Architectural History of Worcester County, Maryland.* Snow Hill, MD: Worcester County Commissioners, 1994.

Townsend, George Alfred. "The Chesapeake Peninsula." *Scribner's Monthly,* March 1872.

BIBLIOGRAPHY

Trapani, Bob, Jr. *Delaware Lights, A History of the Lighthouses in the First State.* Charleston, SC: The History Press, 2007.

———. *Indian River Life-Saving Station...Journey along the Sands.* Virginia Beach: Delaware Seashore Foundation, 2002.

Truitt, Reginald V. *Assateague...the "Place Across": A Saga of Assateague Island.* College Park: University of Maryland Press, 1971.

Truitt, Reginald V., and Millard G. Les Callette. *Worcester Count Maryland's Arcadia.* Snow Hill, MD: Waverly Press, 1977.

Turner, C.H.B., ed. *Some Records of Sussex County.* Philadelphia: Allen, Lane and Scott, 1909.

Vincent, Francis. *A History of the State of Delaware.* Philadelphia: John Campbell, 1870.

Wells, John T., and Charles H. Peterson. *Restless Ribbons of Sand.* Chapel Hill, NC: Institute of Marine Sciences.

Weslager, C.A. *The Siconese Indians of Lewes, Delaware: A Historical Account of a "Great" Bayside Lenape Tribe.* Lewes: Lewes Historical Society, 1991.

The Written Record of the Voyage of 1524 of Giovanni da Verrazano as recorded in a letter to Francis I, King of France, July 8th, 1524. http://bc.barnard.columbia.edu/~lgordis/earlyAC/documents/verrazan.htm.

Newspapers

Baltimore Evening Sun: February 15, 1940.
Baltimore Patriot: February 12, 1831.
Baltimore Sun: July 4, 1937; April 21, 1947; July 5, 1953; July 1, 1958; August 8, 1985.
Beachcomber: February 19, 1982; August 19, 1983; March 16, 1984.
Cape Gazette: September 25, 2017.
Chincoteague Island Chronicle: July 31, 1986.
Connecticut Gazette: December 24, 1790.
Delaware Coast News: November, 20, 1931; January 5, 1932; August 25 and September 1, 1933; July 6, 1934; January 1, August 2, and December 22, 1935; December 12, 1940; October 10 and December 5 and 12, 1941; January 30, February 6, May 1, August 21 and October 2, 1942; February 26 and March 26, 1943; September 12, 1944; August 21, 1946; March 17, 1949; March 1, 8, 15 and 22, 1962; March 7, 2012.
Delaware Coast Press: March 8, 1962; May 18, 1983.

Bibliography

Delaware Pilot: September 12, September 19, 1903.
Delaware State News: June 27, 1976.
Delaware Wave: August 27, 2013.
Democratic Messenger: March 17, 1888; September 14, 1889; September 19, 1903.
Eastern Shore Times: March 24, 1936.
Evening Sun: June 10, 1985.
Maryland Coast Dispatch: August 16, 2013.
New York Times: February 14, 1883; November 28 and 29, 1884; March 13, 14 and 15, 1888; September 11 and 14, 1889; January 4 and 5, 1914; June 4 and 5, 1918; June 6 and 11, 1923; January 3 and 4, 1925; March 21, 1926; August 24 and September 9, 1933; July 25, 1943; August 18, 1946; March 17, 1949; January 20, 1952.
Niles Register: December 17, 1825.
Ocean City Times: October 2, 1985.
Public Press: September 5, 1946; February 12, 1948.
Rehoboth Beacon: April 1876.
Salisbury Times: March 4, 1943.
Smyrna Times: March 14 and March 18, 1888.
Sussex Countian: February 12, 1948.
Washington Post: August 23, 2013.
Wilmington Evening Journal: March 7, 8, 9, 10, 11 and 13, 1962.
Wilmington Morning News: March 8, 9, 10 and 15, 1962.

INDEX

A

Ackerman, Leon 97, 98, 100
Alexander, John H. 67
American Revolution 25, 27, 68, 69
Paradise for Gunners and Anglers, A 63, 66, 69
Argall, Samuel 12
Assateague Island 7, 9, 10, 18, 19, 21, 29, 42, 51, 61, 63, 64, 66, 67, 69, 70, 71, 81, 89, 92, 96, 97, 98, 99, 100, 123, 124, 126, 127, 129
Assateague Island National Seashore 123, 124, 126
Assawoman Bay 74
Atlantic Hotel 44, 61
Atlantic Sands Motel 114

B

Baltimore Boulevard 97, 100
Barlow, Thomas 16, 17
barrier islands 5, 9, 10, 12, 14, 15, 16, 18, 21, 53, 62, 71, 97, 125, 130
beach replenishment 126, 127, 129, 130, 131

Belhaven 114
Berlin 102
Bethany Beach 73, 81, 88, 89, 92, 93, 94, 97, 103, 105, 119, 124, 126
Blackbeard (Edward Teach) 18
Blackiston, Naathaniel 18
Bottle and Cork 111
Bowers Beach 116
Breakwater, Delaware 29, 30, 31, 33, 34, 36, 38, 40, 41, 42, 44, 45, 47, 49, 52, 74, 130
Brown, Nona 103
Bryan Army Air Field 86, 87
Buck, D. Douglass 76
Buck, Frank H. 122

C

Cape Hatteras 23, 35, 72, 88, 125
Cape Henlopen 5, 7, 10, 11, 12, 16, 18, 22, 23, 24, 28, 29, 30, 33, 36, 38, 40, 42, 44, 46, 48, 49, 68, 74, 78, 79, 80, 81, 85, 89, 96, 97, 99, 115, 130
Cape Henlopen Lighthouse 17, 24, 26, 59, 60

INDEX

Cape Henlopen State Park 127
Carter, Richard 94
Chesapeake Bay Bridge 91, 92, 93, 94, 96, 97, 103, 111
Chincoteague Bay 99
Chincoteague Island 5, 10, 18, 19, 66, 67, 72, 97, 99
Chincoteague National Wildlife Refuge 97
Church, Melville 51
Clampitt, John A. 38, 39, 40
Coast Guard 74, 95, 96, 110
Coffin, Isaac 61
Coggeshall, George 30
Congress Hall 44, 51
Corkran, William 75
Cox, Samuel Sullivan 36
Crowell, John S., Jr. 33, 34, 36, 38, 39, 40, 42
Curly 109, 110

D

de Vries, David 23, 46
Dewey Beach 41, 55, 78, 88, 89, 95, 96, 110, 111, 118
Dobson, Stewart 125
Dolle's Candyland 115
Duckworth, Joe 86, 87

F

Fenwick Island 11, 13, 16, 67, 78, 81, 88, 89, 91, 92, 97, 102, 103, 104, 119, 124
Fenwick Island Lighthouse 102, 103, 104
Fish and Wildlife Service 97
fish processing plants 27, 29, 74
Fort Miles 81
Franklin, Benjamin 59
Funland 115

G

Great Dune 11, 23, 24, 47, 78, 79, 80
Green, William E. 98
Groot, Johan J. 123, 132

H

Hall, Richard 91, 92, 93
Harbor of Refuge 45, 49, 52
Hedgecock, John 25
Henlopen Hotel 74, 76, 114
Henry, Marguerite 99
Hill, Thomas 59
Horner, Garnett D. 105
Horn's Pavilion 54, 55
Hudson, Henry 11, 12, 22
Huony, Daniel 19
hurricane hunters 87, 99
hurricanes (defined) 14

I

Indian River Inlet Bridge 78, 95, 128
inlets 64, 69
   Chincoteague 66, 67
   Green Run 69
   Indian River 16, 41, 42, 64, 67, 78, 89, 94, 95, 108, 109, 110, 127, 128
   Ocean City 74, 78, 100
   Sinepuxent 10, 11, 67, 68, 69
Iron Pier 80
Isle of Wight Bay 74

J

Jones-Burdick, William 87

K

Keenwick West 103
Kelley, Harry 126
Kent General Hospital 118
Kidd, William 18

INDEX

Kimball, Summer 36
Kyle, Mary Pat 103, 104

L

Lake Gerar 115
Lewes 16, 17, 18, 22, 24, 27, 29, 33, 38, 39, 40, 42, 47, 51, 59, 68, 74, 80, 85, 89, 116, 118
Lewes Beach 17, 27, 51, 52, 74, 89, 96, 115
Lewes Creek 17, 22, 23, 27
Lewes-Rehoboth Canal 85
Life-Saving Service 31, 35, 63
Life-Saving Stations
  Assateague Island 41
  Bethany Beach 33
  Cape Henlopen 31, 36, 40, 42
  Fenwick Island 33
  Green Run 69
  Indian River Inlet 33, 36, 41, 110
  Lewes 31, 36, 38, 40, 42
  Rehoboth Beach 33, 36, 40, 41
Lord Baltimore 23
Ludlam, Christopher 63, 64

M

Mabry, Bill 109, 110
Marsh, John J. 95
McKeldin, Theodore R. 91
menhaden 27, 28, 63
Merryman, John 40
Methodist Camp Meeting Association 53
Milford, Delaware 35, 42
Milton 116
Misty 99

N

National Guard 102, 108, 110, 116, 118
National Harbor of Refuge 44

National Park Service 96, 97, 98, 124
Native Americans 10, 14, 15, 22, 23, 131
New York 22, 27, 34, 35, 36, 42, 91
nor'easters (defined) 14
North Beach 68

O

Ocean Beach 97, 98, 100, 123
Ocean City 5, 42, 51, 53, 61, 62, 63, 64, 66, 67, 69, 70, 72, 73, 74, 76, 77, 78, 81, 90, 91, 92, 93, 94, 96, 97, 98, 100, 102, 103, 108, 119, 123, 125, 126, 129, 130
O'Hair, Ralph 87
Overton, Jim 109

P

Pearson, Vohnnie 122
Penn, William 24
Philadelphia 12, 16, 24, 27, 29, 33, 34, 52, 63, 68, 95
Pink Pony 113
pirates 49, 68
Plimhimon 51
ponies 5, 19, 29, 63, 66, 70, 99
pound fishing 64, 75
Power, F. D. 93
Prettyman, Solomon 27
Public Landing 66
Pyle, Howard 5, 19, 49, 51

Q

quarantine station 33

R

Rehoboth Bay 111
Rehoboth Beach 5, 13, 15, 16, 51, 53, 54, 55, 57, 59, 60, 67, 70, 73, 74, 75, 76, 77, 78, 79, 85, 86,

INDEX

88, 89, 90, 92, 94, 95, 96, 97, 103, 110, 111, 113, 114, 115, 118, 119, 121, 124, 126
Rhode Island Inn 61
Ringler brothers 81
Ringler Theater 81
Roosevelt, Franklin 64
Route 14 121

S

Salmons, Theodore 40
Scott's Ocean House 69
ships
  Allie H. Belden 33, 34, 36, 38, 39, 40, 42
  Brilliant 30
  Eastern 57
  Faithful Steward 16
  Friendship 16, 17
  General Mifflin 68, 69
  Greyhound 19
  Hattie A. Marsh 52
  La Dauphine 9, 10, 11
  Maud S. 52
  Merrimac 57, 85
  Neiman 94
  Seabird 52
  Severn 57
  Thomas Tracy 85, 86, 88
  Western Prince 72
Siconese 22
Silver Lake 73, 74, 76, 115
Sinepuxent Bay 5, 42, 61, 63, 74, 91
Smith, John 28
Snow Hill 19, 35, 44, 66
Sorin, Herman 102
South Beach 68
South Bethany 92, 93, 104, 105
South Ocean City 96
Spears, John R. 46, 48, 49
storms
  1667 15
  1693 16
  1749 16
  1785 16
  1821 16
  1831 17
  1888 (Ice Storm, Great White Hurricane) 42, 45, 88, 130
  1889 42, 44
  1903 (Vagabond Hurricane) 51, 52, 61, 88, 131
  1914 54, 75, 126
  1918 57
  1920 69
  1928 69
  1933 77, 103, 130
  1944 (Great Atlantic Hurricane) 85, 88, 103
  1950 (Hurricane Carol) 88
  1954 (Hurricane Hazel) 88
  1955 (Hurricane Connie) 88
  1956 (Hurricane Flossy) 88
  1960 (Hurricane Donna) 88
  1961 89
  1962 125
  1962 (Ash Wednesday) 118, 128, 130, 131
  1962, November 124
  1985 (Hurricane Gloria) 125
Stuart Kingston Galleries 114
Stubbs, Enoch 53
Surf Avenue 53, 54, 55, 126
Sussex Apartments 113
Swanendael 22, 23

T

Tabernacle (Auditorium) 93
Tawes, J. Millard 123
Taylor, Bayard 19, 70
towers, observation (spotting) 80
Townsend, George Alfred 30, 33
Truxton, Thomas 40

INDEX

V

Veazey, Thomas Ward 67
Verrazano, da Giovanni 9, 10, 11, 12, 14, 18, 24, 34, 66, 130
Vickers, Washington 41, 42

W

Wallops Island 130
Waples, William E. 17
War of 1812 27, 94
Waterman, G. 27
Waters, Alisa 118
Waters, Eugene 118
Waters, John A. 116
Waters, John, Jr. 118
Whitefield, George 24
Whittington, Mamie 118
Whittington, William 18
Wilson, Charles 18
Windrift hotel 92
Wirth, Conrad 96
Wise, Lester 102

About the Author

The author on the Ocean City beach. *Photo by Thomas Morgan.*

Michael Morgan has been writing freelance newspaper articles about the history of coastal Delaware for over three decades. He is the author of the "Delaware Diary," which appears weekly in the *Delaware Coast Press*, and the "Sussex Journal," which is a weekly feature of the *Wave*. Morgan has also published articles in *Delaware Beach Life*, *America's Civil War*, the *Baltimore Sun*, *Chesapeake Bay Magazine*, *Civil War Times*, *Maryland Magazine*, *World War II Magazine* and other national publications. His "Lore of Delmarva" weekly radio commentary on historical topics relating to the Maryland and Delaware coasts is broadcasted by station WGMD FM 92.7. Morgan's look at history is marked by a lively storytelling style that has made his writing and lectures popular. Morgan is also the author of *Pirates & Patriots: Tales of the Delaware Coast*, *Rehoboth Beach: A History of Surf & Sand*, *Bethany Beach: A Brief History*, *Ocean City: Going Down the Ocean*, *Civil War Delaware: The First State Divided*, *Hidden History of Lewes*, *Delmarva's Patty Cannon: The Devil on the Nanticoke* and *World War II and the Delaware Coast*.

www.ingramcontent.com/pod-product-compliance
Lightning Source LLC
Chambersburg PA
CBHW042140160426
43201CB00021B/2353